ROOTS

THE UNDERGROUND COOKBOOK

Barbara Grunes
and
Anne Elise Hunt

CHICAGO
REVIEW
PRESS

For our grandmothers

Illustrations by Jennifer Elaine Koury

Library of Congress Cataloging-in-Publication Data

Grunes, Barbara.
    Roots : the underground cookbook / Barbara Grunes and Anne
Elise Hunt. — 1st ed.
        p.   cm.
    Includes index.
    ISBN 1-55652-174-X (pbk.) : $9.95
    1. Cookery (Vegetables)   2. Root crops.   I. Hunt, Anne Elise.
II. Title.
TX801.G729   1993
641.6′51—dc20   92-44583
                                                                        CIP

Published by Chicago Review Press, Incorporated
814 North Franklin
Chicago, Illinois 60610

ISBN 1-55652-174-X

CONTENTS

INTRODUCTION

Root vegetables look like something left over from prehistoric times, which indeed they are. Many have strange shapes, wild hairy surfaces, and earthy smells. Roots with smoother skins and more familiar flavors, like potatoes, onions, and carrots, are widely known but generally considered ordinary, everyday food.

Today, Americans are taking a new look at "ordinary, everyday" food. We're going back to basics and redefining them. We want meat loaf and mashed potatoes like Mom used to cook (or like we wish she had cooked), but we want it without the salt and fat. We want carrots and onions and turnips with holiday meals, but we want them without heavy cream sauces. Thanksgiving isn't Thanksgiving unless there are sweet potatoes—but skip the marshmallows, please! We want to prepare meals that will bring pleasure to our family and friends, but we don't want to spend all day cooking. This book is about new ways of fixing ordinary and everyday, unusual and special occasion, root vegetable dishes that are tasty and healthy. Traditional recipes have been modified wherever possible to contain less butter, sugar, and salt.

Between the two of us, we have more than 40 years of experience in the food business. Never before in our professional careers has the interest in health and nutrition been greater. But gone are the restrictive lists of "Don'ts." Today's healthy food is fresh, tasty, and innovative. The challenge to food professionals like us is to come up with recipes that have flavor and flair *and* fit into healthy patterns of eating.

On a more personal note, we both have middle-aged midriffs and high cholesterol levels. And given our family histories, can high blood pressure be far behind? It is clear that we cannot take our health for granted! Preparing foods that are better for ourselves and for our families and friends, we use ingredients and cooking techniques that balance taste and nutrition.

- Seasoning—In traditional cooking, much of the flavor comes from fat. In our recipes, flavor comes from herbs and spices, savory vinegars, tangy citrus juices, and ingredients that pack a big flavor whollop like garlic, peppers, and ginger. We've created exciting new tastes by combining vegetables with piquant fruits and tasty nuts.

- Cheese—Fat-reduced hard and semihard cheeses have limited use in recipes because they don't melt well. By using moderate amounts of full-flavored cheeses like aged cheddar, Parmesan, Jarlsberg, and goat cheese, we get as much or more flavor than we would if we used a greater amount of a milder cheese.

- Fats and oils—Nutrition experts tell us to reduce fat, especially saturated fat, in the food we eat. This is not a low-fat cookbook, but we have reduced fat when possible. Our recipes call for nonstick vegetable spray and minimal fat to sauté and stir-fry. We use primarily margarine and canola and olive oils, which are lower in saturated fat and higher in monounsaturated fat than other oils, shortenings, or butter. Monounsaturated fats are helpful in reducing blood cholesterol levels.

- Eggs—In keeping with current recommendations, we've cut back on egg yolks, increased egg whites, and modified traditional recipes that use a lot of eggs. For food safety, all eggs in our recipes are cooked. Thus, instead of homemade mayonnaise, we used commercial mayonnaise.

- Milk—In most cases, you can use whatever milk you have on hand in the recipes. Cream sauces made with skim milk won't be as white as those made with whole milk, but it's up to you to decide whether calories and fat or appearance is more important; the flavor nuances are hardly noticeable. Where a richer milk is called for, we suggest evaporated skim milk. Many of our recipes are made with reduced-fat yogurt. We've substituted Neufchâtel cream cheese and sour half-and-half for the full-fat varieties of these products.

- Sodium—Because individuals have very different taste preferences for saltiness, we cook with minimal amounts of salt these days and let people add more, if they want. We prefer light soy sauce, which is lower in sodium than regular soy sauce. You won't find garlic salt or celery salt in the lists of ingredients. Instead of salt, we added lemon juice, wine, or vinegar, sometimes balanced with a little sugar.

- Meat—This is a book about vegetables, but it is not intended to be a vegetarian cookbook. Most of our recipes that include meat use lean cuts. We like to combine meat with vegetables and starches, as in stir-fry mixtures and stews. Sometimes we add small amounts of ham, bacon, or prosciutto for flavor; you can omit them if you wish. Meat, served in sensible portion sizes, can be part of a nutritional diet. It is an excellent source of iron, a mineral that is especially needed by women and adolescents. A balanced diet, based on nutrient needs over several days, has a much higher proportion of grains and starches, fruits and vegetables, than meat, fish, or poultry.

- Cooking methods—A traditional root vegetable recipe typically reads, "Peel, put in a pot, and cook in boiling salted water until done, about 1 hour." Any water-soluble or heat-sensitive vitamins end up in the cooking water rather than in the vegetable! Our updated root preparations maximize vitamin retention. We serve vegetables raw, crisp-cooked, steamed, baked in their skins, stir-fried, and grilled. When we cook vegetables in liquid, we often serve the nutrient-rich liquid as part of the dish.

- Texture, shape, and color—We eat with our eyes as well as our mouths. Carrots, beets, sweet potatoes, and radishes have wonderful deep colors that bring out the artist in us. White roots can be combined with fresh herbs, colorful peppers, pimento, or scallion (green onion) tops. The crisp, juicy flesh of jicama is almost fruit-like. Other root vegetables, like sweet potato, turnip, and celeriac (celery root), which are usually cooked, have a surprisingly sweet flavor when eaten raw. Chopping, julienning, shredding, and mashing gives roots entirely different characteristics that offer creative cooks an amazing culinary palette.

Roots of Good Nutrition

Root vegetables fit the recommended nutritional profile: within their high-fiber structures, they store complex carbohydrates, protein, vitamins, and minerals in a tidy, low-fat, low-calorie package.

Carrots and sweet potatoes are top-of-the-list vegetable sources of vitamin A. A half cup of baked sweet potato has almost 2,500 retinol equivalents of the vitamin, and an equal amount of cooked carrots packs a mighty 1,900 retinol equivalents, enough for two or three days. (The recommended daily intake is 800 retinol equivalents for women and 1,000 for men.)

Potatoes, sweet potatoes, turnips, and parsnips are among the best root vegetable sources of vitamin C. Eating vegetables raw maximizes their vitamin C content, since about 30 percent of the vitamin is destroyed by heat. Thin slices of sweet potatoes are a delicious, crunchy low-fat alternative to crackers and chips.

The green tops of beets, turnips, scallions, and leeks contribute some calcium and iron to the diet. Oxalic acid in the greens reduces calcium absorption, however, so don't rely on greens to keep your bones and teeth strong. The iron in greens is not as well absorbed as the iron in meat. With the exception of Jerusalem artichoke, which has 2.55 milligrams of iron, no root vegetable has more than 1 milligram of iron. The Recommended Dietary Allowance (RDA) for iron is 10 milligrams for men, 15 milligrams for women, and 30 milligrams for pregnant women. To boost the absorption of the iron in vegetables, add a source of vitamin C, such as tomatoes or citrus fruit, or prepare them in cast iron cookware. Eating some meat with the greens also increases the absorption of the iron in vegetables.

Root vegetables appear on lists of recommended foods to prevent disease. Cruciferous vegetables (so named because they have cross-shaped flowers) help ward off cancer. Cruciferous roots include turnips, rutabagas, radishes, and horseradish. Beta carotene, the pigment that gives carrots and sweet potatoes their color, is an antioxidant that helps protect against cancer and heart disease. Following the National Cancer Institute guidelines, we should have about 6 milligrams of beta carotene a day. A carrot a day, with 3 to 6 milligrams of beta carotene, may do more than an apple to keep the doctor away! Credit the fiber in roots for helping to lower cholesterol, stabilize blood sugar, and control weight. Carrots are more effective than bran as a "bulking agent." Bran absorbs about five times its weight in water, while raw carrots absorb 20 to 30 times their weight in water.

Americans eat more potatoes than any other vegetable. Most of all, we love french fries and potato chips. With 10 calories per chip and 15 calories per fry, plus the fat absorbed during cooking, they've given potatoes an unfavorable nutrition reputation. Other methods of preparing potatoes, however, enhance the vegetable's excellent complex carbohydrate, high-fiber, no-fat profile. Potatoes are an economical, versatile source of protein, iron, potassium, and vitamin C. A half cup of boiled potatoes has only 67 calories, while a medium baked potato has 110—before butter, sour cream, and other potentially fat-laden toppings. Regularly replace your dull peeler with a sharp new one. With a sharp blade, you can peel a potato (or carrot) without disturbing the nutrient-dense flesh just under the skin.

Virtually anyone who eats five or more servings of vegetables and fruits a day is probably getting the recommended amounts of vitamins A and C, potassium, and fiber. (A serving is generally a half cup.) Root vegetables expand the choices in the vegetable category.

Men and women cannot live on rutabagas and beets alone, but roots have played a major role in helping the fittest to survive. In ancient times, humans ate roots when the hunters had a bad day. Our ancestors in colder climates cultivated and harvested root vegetables to see them through the winter. The race has survived on food, not vitamin pills and supplements! Your skin may take on an orangish cast if you eat too many carrots, but the effect is temporary and harmless. A megadose of vitamin A, on the other hand, can be toxic.

MAJOR NUTRIENTS IN ROOT VEGETABLES*

Vegetable	Calories	Vitamin A (800-1,000 RE)	Vitamin C (60 mg)	Calcium (800-1,200 mg)	Potassium (2,000 mg)	Fiber (25-30 g)
Beets, boiled	26	1	5	9	266	0.72
Carrots, raw	24	1,547	5	15	178	0.57
Carrots, boiled	35	1,915	2	24	115	0.78
Celery root, raw	31	0	6	34	234	1.01
Daikon radish, cooked	13	0	11	12	211	0.36
Horseradish, raw	6	76	5	0	34	0.20
Gingerroot, raw (¹/₄ cup)	17	0	1	4	100	0.25
Jerusalem artichokes, raw	57	2	3	10	NA	0.60
Jicama, raw	25	0	12	9	105	0.42
Leeks, boiled	16	2	2	16	46	0.42
Lotus root, boiled	59	0	24	23	323	0.76
Onions, raw	27	0	7	20	124	0.35
Parsnips, raw	50	0	11	24	251	1.34
Parsnips, boiled	63	0	10	29	286	1.72
Potatoes, boiled, peeled	67	0	6	6	256	0.29
Radishes, raw	10	0	13	12	134	0.32
Rutabagas, boiled	29	0	19	36	244	0.89
Salsify, boiled	46	0	3	32	192	1.01
Scallions (green onions), raw	13	250	23	30	128	0.42
Shallots, raw (1 tablespoon)	7	NA	1	4	33	0.07
Sweet potatoes, raw	72	1,375	16	16	139	0.58
Sweet potatoes, boiled	103	2,182	25	28	348	0.80
Turnips, raw	18	0	14	20	124	0.59
Turnips, boiled	14	0	9	18	106	0.55
Water chestnuts, raw	66	0	3	7	362	0.50

*Root vegetables contain small amounts of other vitamins and minerals as well as carbohydrates and protein. Recommended daily intake for adults is given in parentheses.
†Values are a half cup unless specified otherwise.
Nutrient chart information from U.S. Department of Agriculture, Human Nutrition Information Service, Agriculture Handbook Number 8–11, *Composition of Foods: Vegetables and Vegetable Products*. (rev. ed.) by Washington, D.C.: U.S. Government Printing Office, 1984.

Selecting and Storing Roots

In organizing the book, we wanted, first, to expand your knowledge and cooking repertoire with common root vegetables such as potatoes, carrots, beets, garlic, and onions. Second, we want to revive the use of old-time root cellar vegetables that have gone out of style, such as turnips, parsnips, rutabagas, and parsley root. And third, we want to introduce you to roots that may not be part of your ethnic heritage or culinary experience, such as lotus root, fresh horseradish, jicama, and salsify.

The book has more recipes for the roots that are widely available and one or two recipes for the more unusual ones. Taro, arrowroot, cassava, and tropical yams, which are hard to find, are not included.

The accompanying chart gives information that will help you select root vegetables used in the recipes, as well as helpful tips on storage. Duplicate the chart and take it with you to the market. Because there is a lot of information on potatoes and onions, expanded tables for those vegetables are found in the chapters devoted to them.

We transferred notes from our testing sheets and included tips and serving suggestions. We've also shared some of the fascinating history and background we discovered about the vegetables. Folklore about roots is particularly colorful (and sometimes X-rated).

ROOT VEGETABLES: A SELECTION AND STORAGE GUIDE

Vegetable	Description	Selection	Storage
Beets (¼ pound/serving)	Most common form is deep red, but yellow and white varieties are also available. Green tops are edible.	Fresh, prime beets should have rounded shape, 1½–2 inches in diameter; larger may be woody. Look for firm skin, deep color (if red). Often sold in bunches with greens removed. Greens deteriorate quickly and do not indicate quality of beet root.	Cut off tops immediately, leaving at least ½-inch stem; do not trim root. This will keep red juice from leaking out. Refrigerate unwashed in plastic bag, 7–10 days. Cooked beets keep 3–5 days. To freeze: Scrub, then boil or bake until done; remove skins. Freeze sliced or whole for 10–12 months.
Carrots (1 pound = 3–4 servings)	Bright orange roots with or without feathery tops in a variety of shapes and sizes	Unless very fresh, carrots with tops are less nutritious because tops draw moisture. Avoid soft, shriveled carrots or ones with yellow tops or small green shoots on top. Darker colored carrots have more vitamin A than lighter ones. Discard green-tinged ends.	Cut off tops and refrigerate in plastic bag, or leave trimmed carrots in bag and refrigerate up to 2 weeks. Use wilted carrots in stew or soup. Avoid contact with apples, which cause carrots to turn bitter. To freeze: Blanch whole for 5 minutes, or sliced for 2 minutes. Freeze 10–12 months.
Celery root, or Celeriac (1 pound whole = ½ pound peeled)	A gnarled round clump with roots at one end and short green stalks at the other. Scrape with fingernail—it will smell like celery. It tastes like celery but is nuttier. Its texture is crisp. Can be eaten raw or cooked.	Choose a small to medium bulb with few roots. The smoother the skin, the easier to peel. Stalk end should be firm.	Trim off roots and tops. Refrigerate in plastic bag for 3–4 days.

ROOT VEGETABLES: A SELECTION AND STORAGE GUIDE (continued)

Vegetable	Description	Selection	Storage
Gingerroot	A gnarled tuber with small sprouts on the sides. Young ginger, usually available only in Asian stores, is pinkish with a soft skin. Ginger has a sharp flavor; the young sprouts are milder than the main tuber.	Choose root section that is firm and plump with new sprouts on sides. These new spouts are more delicate in flavor than the main root.	Refrigerate, tightly wrapped, in plastic wrap for 2–3 weeks. Freeze unpeeled ginger in airtight plastic bag 4 weeks. Refrigerate, covered with white wine or sherry in covered jar up to 6 months. Pour off wine for dressings; replace with new wine. In all cases, slice off what you need and return unused portion.
Horseradish	A woody yellow-brown root, usually cut into lengths. Can be distinguished by smell. Flavor is stronger when fresh.	Choose a very firm piece with white flesh. Avoid roots with greenish tint or sprouts.	Refrigerate in plastic bag up to 3 weeks. Scrape off any soft spots or mold that may develop.
Jerusalem artichokes, or sunchokes	Bumpy brown tubers (actually roots of a variety of sunflower) with white flesh. Usually packaged by Frieda of California. They have a crisp texture, something like a water chestnut, and a mild, clean flavor that, to some, resembles artichoke heart. They cause flatulence in some individuals.	Choose smooth, unblemished tubers with the fewest protrusions. Avoid those that have a greenish tint or are sprouting.	Refrigerate in plastic bag for up to 2 weeks. Do not freeze.

Vegetable	Description	Selection	Storage
Jicama (pronounced "hee-cama")	A large smooth-skinned tuber that resembles a potato. It ranges in size from 8 ounces to 5 pounds. Has crisp texture and slightly sweet, bland flavor similar to water chestnut. (It can be substituted for water chestnuts in recipes.) Some have watery juice; others a milky juice. Does not discolor when cut.	Large size may be woody. Choose firm, smooth, thin-skinned root (scratch to test). May have some blemishes. Starchier jicama can be cooked; others may be eaten raw or cooked.	Refrigerate whole, unwrapped, up to 2 weeks. Wrap tightly after cutting and store in refrigerator up to a week.
Onions, leeks, shallots, and garlic: See charts in chapter.			
Parsley root	Small, beige-colored, carrot-shaped root with parsley leaves. Tastes slightly herbal.	Choose firm, light-colored roots. Small to medium-sized are best.	Refrigerate untrimmed in plastic bag up to 2 weeks.
Parsnips (1 pound = 2 servings)	Looks like an ivory-colored carrot, with a sweet, nutty flavor.	Choose smooth-skinned parsnips that are free of rootlets. The sweetest parsnips are those that are left in the ground over the winter so that the starch turns to sugar.	Remove tops; refrigerate in plastic bag up to 10 days. To freeze: Wash, peel, cube and blanch 2 minutes; or freeze whole, fully cooked, 8–10 months.
Potatoes: See chart in chapter.			
Radishes	Most common is small "button" red; white icicle, and round white, and large black radishes are also available. Daikon is long, thin white Japanese radish. All are crisp, white, and piquant.	Choose firm, hard radish without cracks or soft spots. Greens do not indicate root quality.	Remove tops before storing. Refrigerate in sealed plastic bag up to 2 weeks. Do not freeze.

ROOT VEGETABLES: A SELECTION AND STORAGE GUIDE (concluded)

Vegetable	Description	Selection	Storage
Rutabagas ($^1/_4$ pound = one serving)	Large, round, and smooth-skinned with purplish streaks. Rutabagas are interchangeable with turnips but have a stronger flavor.	Rutabagas should feel heavy and firm. They generally are waxed to prevent dehydration.	Store at room temperature up to 1 week or in plastic bag in refrigerator up to 2 months. To freeze: Freeze cubed, blanched or whole, fully cooked, for 8–10 months.
Salsify, or oyster plant (1 pound = 2 servings)	A long carrot-shaped root with grasslike tops. The more common variety is tan. Black salsify, also called *scorzonera*, has a dark brown skin. Some say salsify tastes like oysters; others say it is more like turnips. Can cause flatulence.	Sold in bunches or plastic bags late fall through early spring. Choose firm, medium-sized roots.	Refrigerate in plastic bag up to 2 weeks. Do not freeze.
Turnips ($^1/_4$ pound = one serving)	Popular variety is white with purplish streaks. Early crops sometimes sold with green tops, which are edible if fresh.	Avoid very large turnips. Choose firm, unwrinkled turnips with smooth skin.	Remove greens; refrigerate greens no longer than 1 week. Refrigerate unwashed turnips in plastic bag 1 week. To freeze: See rutabagas.
Water chestnuts	Bulblike shapes with shaggy brown skins, $1^1/_2$–2 inches in diameter. Sweet flavor something like coconut.	Choose only those that are hard with no soft spots. Avoid any that look shriveled.	Refrigerate unwashed in paper bag or place in a jar of water in the refrigerator for 2 weeks. To freeze: Store unwashed in plastic bag.

Root Cellars Remembered

We remember being sent "down cellar" at Grandmother's house to bring up potatoes or beets from a cold, remote corner under the house. Even now, the smell of roots reminds us of the earthy odor of that mysterious dark place. The area was well fortified with traps to stop hungry mice from invading the supply room. We were terrified of encountering a captured creature! In another part of the cellar (it was never called the basement), there were shelves lined with jars of onions ready to be creamed for Sunday dinner, pickled beets, and dilled carrots.

Roots conjure up memories of times past. In winter, onions with dried tops were laid out on cheesecloth-lined racks in the attic. In an outdoor shed, where their pungent odors wouldn't smell up the cellar, turnips and rutabagas were packed in moist sand. Late potatoes, which are better "keepers" than earlier varieties, were held as long as weather permitted in our northern climes, then moved to the root cellar. There, they spent the winter in crates or baskets, in a dark, cool spot—but never near the apples, and never where they might be exposed to sunlight. Apples "breathe" during storage, and their moisture and odor can spoil potatoes. Sunlight makes potatoes turn green and develop a toxic substance called solanine.

In cold climates, parsnips and salsify can spend the winter in the frozen ground. The earth is piled up over them to prevent an inadvertent thaw. During this hibernation, their starch slowly turns to sugar, and they emerge with a more subtle, sweet flavor. Horseradish, too, is wintered outside. It is uncovered and allowed to freeze, then buried for the duration of the winter.

In root cellars, constant vigilance was essential to be sure the storage areas didn't get too cold, too warm, or too damp. Vegetables were sorted and those that rotted were discarded; sprouts were removed and crops carefully rotated in bins and barrels.

If you live in an older house, there may still be remnants of these earlier times: a room with masonry walls, usually on the north or east side, with packed earth floors and a small window for cross-ventilation. Or you may have an outside cellar entrance with wide doors and cement steps. The steps were often used as a holding area for fruits and vegetables. Snow was piled on the outside door to provide insulation, and a bucket of damp sand added humidity to the area.

Today, you can enjoy root vegetables without getting your hands dirty, putting on your galoshes, or going down into a dark, cold cellar. Cruise down to the local supermarket. Pick up a few turnips or rutabagas, choose from among three or four varieties of potatoes and onions, and check out.

ONE

ASIAN ROOTS

The manner in which Chinese and Japanese cooks use roots warrants a special chapter. In Asian kitchens, lowly sweet potatoes, carrots, radishes, turnips, onions, and garlic are transformed into culinary works of art. Fresh water chestnuts and sliced lotus root expand the repertoire, and fresh gingerroot offers complex flavor possibilities.

Asian food and cooking methods are well suited to today's lifestyle. Health-conscious individuals have learned the benefits of its low-fat, high-flavor dishes. Busy people have discovered the value of quick and easy stir-frying. We hope that our recipes will convince you to explore or expand your Asian food preparation skills.

Here, and in the following chapters, you will find Asian inspired root recipes. Fresh water chestnuts, lotus root, and ginger are identified more closely with Japanese and Chinese cooking than other roots. Cassava (also called yucca, manioc, and tapioca) and taro (the basis of Hawaii's fermented *poi*) are hard to find and are therefore not included in this book.

For years, we've been eating canned water chestnuts in rumaki, chop suey, and spinach salad. Eating fresh water chestnuts is a very different taste experience. They are somewhat crisper and have a much more pronounced flavor than the canned variety. They taste a little like coconut or a sweet apple. Water chestnuts are appropriately named—they do look like chestnuts, and they grow in the water. They are, in fact, bulbs or corms that are similar to a narcissus bulb, and they have a thin, dark brown skin.

Fresh water chestnuts can be peeled either before or after cooking. They stay whiter if they are cooked without the peel. Use a very sharp knife to remove the skins, then drop them into sugar water to help preserve their natural sweetness. Don't let them soak for long, however, as they will absorb water. Boil or steam fresh water chestnuts 10 to 15 minutes, and serve them hot with melted margarine or butter and salt and pepper. Or add them, either raw or parboiled, to give crunch to recipes.

Lotus root is the long, brown tuberous root of an Asian water lily. The lily produces lovely white and pink flowers. The root yields a crisp-textured starchy vegetable somewhat like a potato but with a sweeter taste. Lotus root is valued for its unusual appearance. Air passages that run the length of the root make an attractive lacy design when it's cut crosswise.

Gingerroot is widely used in Asian recipes and medicines. Chinese sailors in the fifth century carried ginger to ward off scurvy. While the root is not an outstanding source of scurvy-preventing vitamin C, modern-day studies substantiate the claim that gingerroot prevents motion sickness, a more common problem than scurvy for today's seafarers. Research is under way to explore the root's natural antioxidant qualities in relation to heart disease, cancer, and aging.

During the Middle Ages, ginger was widely used to boost the flavor of weak winter soups and stews. Depending on its preparation, ginger can be sweet, hot, or bitter. Chinese cooks preserve ginger in sweet syrup, pickle it in vinegar, and combine it with salty soy. Cooking gingerroot modifies its flavor. Add it at the end of cooking time if you want to take advantage of its hot properties.

Substituting dried, powdered gingerroot for fresh gingerroot is not recommended. Fresh ginger has a sharp, pungent flavor that is quite different from the dried variety. If you do choose to make the substitution, measure $1/4$ teaspoon of dried, powdered ginger for each teaspoon of fresh, grated gingerroot. Keep a piece of gingerroot in the freezer, tightly wrapped in plastic wrap. Scrape away the peel on the amount you need and grate the frozen root. Wrap and return the rest to the freezer. You can also store unpeeled gingerroot in the refrigerator in a small jar covered with sherry.

To grow your own ginger, place a plump root in a large pot of rich soil, just under the surface. Water and mist when green shoots appear. Begin harvesting ginger when the plant is about 1 year old. Dig up the tender sprouts without disturbing the main root.

Stir-Fried Root Vegetables

6 to 8 servings

2	tablespoons cornstarch
3/4	cup chicken broth
1/3	cup light soy sauce
2	tablespoons light brown sugar
2	tablespoons dry white wine
2	tablespoons hoi-sin sauce*
2	tablespoons canola oil
1	large onion, thinly sliced
3	cloves garlic, minced
1/2	teaspoon grated fresh gingerroot
2	cups peeled, diced turnips
1	cup thinly sliced carrots
1	cup Russet (baking) potatoes, peeled, cubed, parboiled, and drained
1/2	teaspoon salt
1/4	teaspoon freshly ground pepper

Whole-wheat noodles, cooked

Whisk cornstarch and chicken broth in a small bowl. Mix soy sauce, brown sugar, wine, and hoi-sin in a large bowl; stir in cornstarch mixture. Reserve. Heat oil in a wok or heavy frying pan. Stir-fry the onion, garlic, and ginger, cooking quickly over medium-high heat, stirring often with a spatula, for about 30 seconds. Add turnips, carrots, and potatoes; stir-fry for about 4 minutes. Add soy sauce mixture. Cover and cook, stirring occasionally, until vegetables are tender, 3 to 4 minutes. Season with salt and pepper. Serve hot with whole-wheat noodles.

*Available in Asian food stores or large supermarkets.

Beef, Lotus Root, and Scallions

Lotus root comes fresh, dried, or canned. To reconstitute dried lotus root, cover with boiling water and let it stand 30 minutes. Drain and cut in quarters.

6 servings

2	tablespoons canola oil
1/2	teaspoon grated fresh gingerroot
2	cloves garlic, minced
1	pound lotus root, peeled, and cut into 1/4-inch slices (or reconstituted, dried lotus root)*
1	pound flank steak, thinly sliced against the grain
1	cup chopped broccoli
3	tablespoons dry white wine
2	tablespoons light soy sauce
1/2	cup chicken broth, mixed with 2 tablespoons cornstarch
1/2	teaspoon salt
1/4	teaspoon freshly ground pepper
1	cup toasted peanuts
6	scallions, chopped

Hot, cooked brown or white rice

Heat oil in a wok or heavy frying pan over medium-high heat. Stir-fry ginger and garlic; that is, cook quickly over medium-high heat, stirring often with a spatula, for about 30 seconds. Add lotus root, beef, and broccoli. Cook, stirring continually, until beef is brown, about 2 minutes. Reduce heat to medium-low. Add wine, soy sauce, and cornstarch mixture. Cook and stir until meat is tender and sauce has thickened slightly, 2 to 3 minutes. Season with salt and pepper. Spoon onto serving dish. Sprinkle with peanuts and garnish with chopped scallions. Serve hot with cooked brown or white rice.

*Available in Asian food stores or large supermarkets.

Stuffed Pepper Pieces

Water chestnut flour is used in Asian cooking as one would use cornstarch. Water chestnut flour and fresh water chestnuts are available at Asian food stores. Canned water chestnuts are readily available at large supermarkets.

6 servings, 12 pieces

¹/₂	pound lean ground pork
4 to 5	fresh water chestnuts, peeled and minced *or*
1	8-ounce can of water chestnuts, drained and minced
2	scallions, including tender green tops, minced
¹/₂	teaspoon grated fresh gingerroot
2	tablespoons dry white wine
¹/₂	teaspoon salt
3	large red bell peppers, quartered lengthwise
¹/₂	cup cornstarch or water chestnut flour
3	tablespoons canola oil
2	tablespoons light soy sauce
1	teaspoon sugar
¹/₂	cup water

Combine pork, water chestnuts, scallions, gingerroot, wine, and salt in a large bowl. Press some of the pork mixture into each pepper section. Spoon cornstarch onto a plate. Roll stuffing side of pepper strips in cornstarch, coating the top. Heat canola oil in a large heavy skillet. Fry the peppers, stuffing side down, over high heat, 2 minutes. Mix soy sauce, sugar, and water in small a bowl; add to skillet, taking care because it will splatter. Cover and cook until peppers are tender, about 6 minutes. To serve, remove peppers with spatula. Serve stuffing side up, two per person.

Stir-Fried Turnips and Beef

Partially freezing the meat will make it easier to cut it into thin strips. Cut against the grain with a sharp knife.

6 to 8 servings

1/4	cup light soy sauce
1	tablespoon sugar
2	tablespoons dry white wine
2	tablespoons oyster sauce*
2	tablespoons canola oil
1	teaspoon grated fresh gingerroot
2	cloves garlic, minced
4	scallions, including tender green tops, minced
1/2	teaspoon five-spice powder*
1/2	teaspoon salt
1/4	teaspoon freshly ground pepper
3/4	pound turnips, peeled, thinly sliced, parboiled 4 minutes, and drained
1	pound flank steak, thinly sliced
1	15-ounce can baby corn, drained

Whole-wheat noodles, cooked

Mix soy sauce, sugar, wine, and oyster sauce in a small bowl; reserve. Heat oil in a wok or heavy skillet over medium-high heat. Stir-fry the ginger, garlic, scallions, five-spice powder, salt, and pepper, about 30 seconds. Add turnips; stir-fry 2 minutes. Add meat and continue cooking, quickly turning with a spatula, until meat is cooked and loses its pink color. Stir in corn and reserved soy mixture. Cook, stirring constantly, until sauce thickens slightly, about 2 minutes. Serve hot over whole-wheat noodles.

*Available in Asian food stores or large supermarkets.

Sweet Potato and Turnip Pancakes

These pancakes are good as an appetizer, side dish, or lunch dish.

6 to 8 servings

3/4	pound turnips, peeled and grated (about 2 cups)
1	medium-sized sweet potato, peeled and grated (about 1 cup)
1 1/2	cups chicken broth
1	cup all-purpose flour
1/2	cup cornstarch
2	cloves garlic, minced
1	teaspoon grated gingerroot
1/2	teaspoon salt
1/4	teaspoon ground ginger
1/4	teaspoon freshly ground white pepper
2	medium-sized onions, grated
	Canola oil for frying pancakes

Combine grated turnips and sweet potato in a large deep bowl. Stir in chicken broth, flour, cornstarch, garlic, grated and ground ginger, salt, pepper, and onions. Cover and refrigerate at least 2 hours (or overnight).

Heat 6 tablespoons of the oil in a heavy skillet. Stir batter. From each ladle of batter, make two pancakes. Cook on both sides until golden brown and cooked through. Drain on paper toweling. Add more oil as needed. Pancakes may be kept warm in a 275-degree oven, but they are best served fresh and hot off the griddle.

Cantonese Scallion Bread

Two, 10-inch rounds

2	cups all-purpose flour
$1/2$	teaspoon baking powder
$3/4$	cup boiling water
3	tablespoons vegetable shortening
4	scallions, including tender green tops, minced
	Coarse kosher salt
	Flour for rolling out dough
$1/2$	cup canola oil

Mix flour and baking powder in a food processor fitted with steel blade. With the machine running, pour water through the feed tube; mix until a dough ball forms, 6 to 10 seconds. Remove dough ball; divide into two parts. Cover dough with aluminum foil and let stand at room temperature for 1 hour. If dough is sticky, sprinkle with a little flour so it will be manageable.

Knead each piece of dough on a lightly floured board for 1 minute. Roll each as large as possible with a rolling pin. Spread each piece of dough with $1^1/2$ tablespoons of the vegetable shortening. Spoon scallions evenly over dough circles; sprinkle with salt. Roll up jelly-roll style, pulling slightly horizontally as you roll. Beginning at the center, coil each roll into a circular shape. Roll out with a rolling pin into 10-inch rounds. The coils may split as you roll them out.

Heat the oil in a 12-inch skillet over medium heat to 375 degrees. Cook dough rounds, one at a time, turning carefully, until light brown, 10 to 12 seconds on each side. Drain on paper toweling. Serve hot; cut each bread round into eight wedges with kitchen scissors. This bread freezes well.

Pickled Ginger

When we are at our local Japanese restaurant, they know to give us an extra portion of pickled ginger with our meal. Pickled ginger is good with roast meats or steamed fish as well as with Asian food.

About 1¹/₂ cups pickled ginger

1¹/₂	cups boiling water
¹/₂	pound gingerroot, peeled and cut into ¹/₈-inch slices
1	cup rice vinegar*
2¹/₂	tablespoons sugar
³/₄	teaspoon salt

Pour boiling water over gingerroot in a small deep bowl. Let stand 45 seconds; drain. Combine vinegar, sugar, and salt in medium-sized non-metallic bowl; stir in drained ginger. Cover with plastic wrap and let stand at room temperature 45 minutes; refrigerate overnight. Serve, drained, in sauce dish.

*Available in Asian food stores or in the Asian section of supermarkets.

Lotus Root and Beef Soup

6 to 8 servings

2	tablespoons canola oil
1¼	pounds trimmed chuck steak, cut into ½-inch pieces
1	teaspoon grated fresh gingerroot
2	cups beef broth
1	pound lotus root, peeled and cut into ¼-inch pieces
2	cups sliced white mushrooms
2	cups trimmed snow peas
4	scallions, including tender green tops, chopped
½	teaspoon salt
¼	teaspoon freshly ground pepper
¼	teaspoon five-spice powder*

Heat oil in a stock pot or Dutch oven. Sear the meat with ginger over medium-high heat, stirring often, until light brown on all sides. Reduce heat and add beef broth, lotus root, mushrooms, snow peas, and scallions. Add water to cover; heat to boiling. Reduce heat; cover and simmer 1½ hours. Season with salt, pepper, and five-spice powder. Taste and adjust seasoning. Add more water or beef broth, if necessary. Serve hot, ladled into bowls. You might want to add some cooked rice or Asian noodles.

*Available in Asian food stores or large supermarkets.

Spicy Shrimp with Water Chestnuts

6 servings

3	tablespoons cornstarch
2	egg whites, slightly beaten
2	teaspoons light soy sauce
$^1/_2$	teaspoon salt
$^1/_4$	teaspoon baking soda
1	tablespoon dry white wine
$1^1/_2$	pounds extra-large shrimp, shelled and deveined

Spicy Sauce

$^1/_4$	cup light soy sauce
3	tablespoons catsup
2	tablespoons dry white wine
4	teaspoons sugar
1	teaspoon vinegar

4 to 6	tablespoons canola oil
$^3/_4$	teaspoon grated fresh gingerroot
3	cloves garlic, minced
4	scallions, including tender green tops, minced
$^1/_2$	teaspoon red pepper flakes
1	8-ounce can sliced water chestnuts, drained

Hot, cooked brown or white rice

Combine cornstarch, egg whites, soy sauce, salt, baking soda, and wine in a medium-sized bowl; toss with shrimp. Let stand at room temperature 1 hour. Meanwhile, make Spicy Sauce: Combine all ingredients in small bowl; reserve.

Heat oil in a wok or heavy skillet over medium heat. Stir-fry shrimp until opaque white; do not overcook as shrimp will become tough. Remove shrimp with a slotted spoon to a plate. Add ginger, garlic, scallions, and red pepper flakes to wok; stir-fry 1 minute. Add water chestnuts. Return shrimp to wok. Stir in reserved Spicy Sauce; cook only until hot, about 1 minute. Serve over hot cooked rice.

Candied Ginger

1³/₄ to 2 cups candied ginger

¹/₂	pound gingerroot, knobs removed, peeled
2¹/₂	cups sugar, divided
1¹/₂	cups water

Cut peeled ginger into thin slices, about the thickness of a quarter; reserve. Mix 2 cups of the sugar into the water in a heavy medium-sized pan. Heat to boiling over high heat. Stir in the ginger. Reduce heat. Simmer uncovered for 1 hour, stirring occasionally. Mixture will become syrupy and ginger will soften. Drain; reserve and refrigerate syrup. Use syrup for Ginger Ice Cream (see Index) or as a flavoring sauce.

Sprinkle remaining sugar on a sheet of aluminum foil. Spread ginger over sugar; turn to coat on all sides. Let ginger dry overnight. Cover and refrigerate until needed.

Ginger Ice Cream

Commercially preserved ginger is a sweet ginger bottled in a decorative green urn with a syrup sauce. It is the base for the easiest and perhaps one of the most delicious desserts. Preserved ginger is available at Asian food stores.

6 servings

12	scoops of premium-quality vanilla ice cream
1	cup chopped Candied Ginger with sweet syrup (see Index)

At serving time, set two scoops of ice cream in each sauce or ice cream dish. Spoon ginger and sauce over ice cream. If you want, you can also serve this dish with sweetened whipped cream, or nondairy whipped topping, and a plain cookie. Serve immediately.

Chinese Sweet Potato Balls

You can substitute canned, drained sweet potatoes for the fresh potatoes. It is not necessary to cook them; just mash and proceed with the recipe. This dessert is good with Asian food or any meal.

6 to 8 servings

1½	pounds sweet potatoes, peeled, quartered, cooked, and drained
⅓	cup sugar
½	cup all-purpose flour
¼	teaspoon salt
1	egg
2	cups canola oil
¼	cup confectioners' sugar

Mash potatoes until smooth in a large deep bowl. Stir in sugar, flour, salt, and egg. Heat oil to 375 degrees in a wok or medium-sized saucepan. Shape potato mixture into walnut-sized balls. Cook in hot oil, about six at a time, until golden brown, about 1 minute. Remove with slotted spoon; drain on paper toweling. Keep warm in 275-degree oven. Serve warm, sprinkled with confectioners' sugar.

TWO

POTATOES

In times past, potatoes, along with other vegetables like peas, carrots, and beans, were considered aphrodisiacs. The word vegetable comes from the Latin *vegetus*, meaning active and lively, and those who ate them were thought to be spirited lovers. Potatoes are a distant relative of the mandrake, a tuber known in ancient Egypt as the "phallus of the field."

What was revered at one time and place was forbidden in another. A 15th-century pope denounced potatoes as an erotic stimulant. During the Renaissance, leprosy, rickets, and warts were blamed on potatoes. They were publicly burned to protect the citizens from their addictive and potentially dangerous properties. Perhaps their common but distant relation to the deadly nightshade plant gave them their bad reputation.

Meanwhile, potatoes were a common food in South America for thousands of years before the conquistadors arrived. Potatoes were, and still are, a dietary staple in Peru. Spanish explorers took some of the ancestral potatoes back to Europe with them, and within 50 years potatoes were widely cultivated on the continent. One acre of potatoes could feed a family for a year. The French adopted the lowly potato and raised it to haute cuisine and haute couture. Marie Antoinette was said to have worn potato flowers in her hair as she dined on *pommes de terre*.

Credit the poor of Germany and Ireland, however, for making potatoes a mainstay in modern diets. A German cookbook published in 1581 contains a dozen potato recipes. Nineteenth century Irish peasants, who ate potatoes for breakfast, lunch, and dinner, were devastated when a blight destroyed the crops in 1845 and 1846. Thousands died of starvation. Others came to America and became such prodigious consumers of this country's potatoes that the vegetable became known as the "Irish potato."

Grocers usually classify potatoes as "baking," "boiling," "all-purpose," and "new." They differ from one another primarily in the amount of starch they contain. Those that are higher in starch are called "mealy" potatoes. Those lower in starch are known as "waxy" potatoes. Russets tend to be mealy and Round Reds, waxy. Long and Round Whites can be either waxy or mealy. To test the density, dunk potatoes in a gallon of water to which you've added a pound of salt. Mealy potatoes will sink, while the waxy ones will float. Some potatoes float midway in the solution and can be used however one wishes.

Mealy potatoes absorb more water during cooking than the less starchy variety and are thus less able to hold a firm shape. They will not brown as evenly as the waxy variety because they contain less sugar. Mealy potatoes are best for baking and mashing. They are also used for french fries and chips. Waxy potatoes are the best choice when you want a firm potato with a sweet taste. They are used for salads, boiled, or pan-roasted potatoes, parsleyed potatoes, and scalloped potatoes.

Though potatoes are associated with the Irish, among the 400 or so varieties of potatoes, there is no such thing as an ''Irish potato.'' On a recent trip to the supermarket, we had our choice of Petit Red, Idaho Russet, Wisconsin Russet, Golden Delight, New Red, Super Spuds, Idaho Baking, Yukon Gold, and B-Size Reds! There are, however, only four main types of potatoes: Russet, Long White, Round White, and Round Red.

New potatoes are not a separate variety but a freshly dug potato. They are most often the firm, waxy type. The best ones are those that are in the market from early spring through the summer. They can be held only a matter of days, whereas more mature potatoes will keep for several weeks in a cool, dark storage area. Some say that potatoes, like bananas, should never be put in the refrigerator, though the ideal keeping temperature is 40 to 50 degrees Fahrenheit. The starch in potatoes changes to sugar in very cool temperatures, and the texture changes somewhat. If you do refrigerate potatoes, remove them and let them stand a day at room temperature before using them.

In preparing potatoes, always scrub them well under cold running water. Cut out any soft or discolored spots, especially those that have a green tint, and sprouts. The green color indicates the possible presence of solanine, a chemical compound that can make you sick if eaten in large amounts. Cooking diminishes the dangers from solanine, but it's best to cut off the suspect portions.

Potatoes discolor when they're peeled unless they are covered with cold water. It's easier simply to bring them to a boil in the cold water, rather than to transfer them to another pot of boiling water. Our cooking times are based on how long it took to cook cut up potatoes in cold water to fork-tenderness. These times vary depending on the density of the potato, how large or small you cut up the potatoes, and the type of cooking pot and stove.

Sweet Potatoes

Sweet potatoes aren't really potatoes but tubers related to the morning glory family. Sweet potatoes are often called "yams," but technically, sweet potatoes and yams are unrelated. The sweet potato is a native of Central America, while the yam is of African origin. In colonial times, African slaves saw a similarity between the native American sweet potato and their *nyami* and renamed the vegetable "yam." Sweet potatoes (yams) have since been a mainstay of African-American cooking. The noted African-American scientist George Washington Carver is said to have recorded 500 ways to prepare the vegetable. To this day, sweet potatoes in Louisiana, Georgia, and North Carolina are more likely to be called yams than sweet potatoes, and canned products produced in the South are labeled as yams. Only nutritionists, who know that a true yam is nutritionally inferior to a sweet potato, will argue about semantics.

Store sweet potatoes in a perforated plastic bag at room temperature for no more than a week. They keep best at 45 to 50 degrees Fahrenheit and can be refrigerated for up to 10 days. Add a little lemon juice to preserve the color before freezing cooked sweet potatoes. Figure 3 to 4 servings to a pound.

The following chart will help you choose the correct potato to use in recipes.

TYPES OF POTATOES AND THEIR USES

Type	Description/Season	Use
Russet; also called Idaho or Bakers	Elongated with reddish-brown skin. Starchy, and therefore flaky, mealy when cooked. Available year-round.	Baking, frying. Allow 1/serving. 2–3 = 1 pound.
Long Whites; also called California Long Whites, White Rose	Elongated with smooth, tan skin. Firmer and more moist than Russets. Considered an all-purpose potato. Available mid-May–mid-September, mid-December–mid-March.	Boiling, frying, mashing, roasting. Allow 1/serving. 3–5 = 1 pound.
Round Whites; also called Maine or Eastern. "Golden" skin potatoes such as Yukon and Golden Delight are a form of Round Whites.	Smooth and round with tan skin. Firmer and more moist than Russets. Considered an all-purpose potato. Available year-round. New potatoes available mid-May–mid-September.	Boiling, steaming, mashing, roasting, frying. Allow 1–2/serving, depending on size. 3–4 = 1 pound.
Round Reds	Smooth and round with red skin. Available year-round; new potatoes best in spring.	Boiling, steaming, roasting. Allow 2–4/serving, depending on size. 4–8 = 1 pound.
Sweet Potatoes; sometimes called a yam, though technically not correct	Two varieties: one pinkish-yellow and a moister, red-orange one. The deeper-colored one has more vitamin A. Choose blemish-free, medium-sized, smooth. Available year-round. Fresh varieties in fall are less sweet than aged ones.	Boiling, steaming, mashing, grilling, roasting. Allow 1/serving. 3–4 = 1 pound.

The potato recipes here include savory dishes and desserts. The savory selection includes salads, side dishes, and main dish recipes for all kinds of white, red, and sweet potatoes. The desserts illustrate how potatoes can be used in breads, muffins, doughnuts, pies, cakes, and even candy!

New Potatoes Steamed over Lemongrass

6 servings

2	stalks lemongrass, chopped*
4	slices fresh gingerroot
2	cloves garlic, mashed
1¹/₂	pounds new red or white potatoes, unpeeled
¹/₄	cup (¹/₂ stick) margarine or butter
1¹/₂	cups unseasoned dry fine bread crumbs
¹/₂	teaspoon dried thyme
	Salt and freshly ground pepper
	Lemongrass or strip of lemon peel for garnish

Place lemongrass, gingerroot, and garlic in the bottom of a steamer. Fill pan three-quarters full with water and bring water to a boil over medium-high heat; boil 3 minutes. Arrange potatoes on a rack over water. Cover; reduce heat and simmer until potatoes are tender, 15 to 20 minutes. While potatoes are steaming, melt margarine in a skillet over medium heat; stir in crumbs. Cook, stirring often, until crumbs are golden brown, about 5 minutes. Season with thyme and salt and pepper to taste.

To serve, place cooked potatoes in a deep bowl; toss with seasoned crumbs. Garnish with a sprig of lemongrass or lemon peel strip. Serve with Welsh Grandma's Pickled Onions (see Index).

*Available in Asian food stores or large supermarkets.
3 tablespoons grated lemon zest may be substituted for the lemongrass.

Hashed Brown Potatoes

Hashed Brown Potatoes can be either cubed or grated before they are fried to a golden brown. The grated potatoes are lacy and light, while the cubed potatoes are heartier. Hashed Brown Potatoes are good as a side dish for eggs, chicken, or meat. If you want, add chopped cooked chicken or turkey for a "skillet pie." This recipe is wonderful made with leftover potatoes.

6 servings

2	tablespoons canola oil
3	tablespoons margarine, butter, or bacon drippings
1	medium-sized onion, chopped (about 1/2 cup)
6	Round Red potatoes, boiled, peeled, and cut into 1/2-inch cubes
1/4	teaspoon celery salt
	Salt
	Freshly ground pepper

Heat oil and margarine in a large heavy skillet over medium heat. Add onion to skillet; cook, stirring occasionally, until onion is soft, about 4 minutes. Add potatoes; cook, stirring occasionally, over medium heat until potatoes are hot and a golden crusty brown. Sprinkle with celery salt; season to taste with salt and pepper.

Potato Dumplings in the German Style

Potato Dumplings are a traditional German dish usually served with meat and gravy. We like them with sauerkraut and roast pork or pot roast.

16 dumplings

6	medium-sized white potatoes, about 2 pounds, peeled, quartered, boiled, and drained
2	eggs, slightly beaten
3/4	cup all-purpose flour
1/2	cup farina or cream of wheat (uncooked)
1	tablespoon finely chopped fresh parsley
1	teaspoon salt
1/4	teaspoon ground cinnamon
1/4	teaspoon ground nutmeg

Put potatoes through a ricer; cool to room temperature. Fill a large deep skillet or Dutch oven with salted water to a depth of 1 1/2 to 2 inches; heat to boiling while preparing dumplings. Place potatoes in a deep bowl; stir in remaining ingredients. Knead dough gently with hands to form a soft dough. Rinse hands with cold water. Form dough into balls, about 1 1/2 inches in diameter; place on a plate or waxed paper until all are formed. Slide dumplings into boiling water. If they do not fit in a single layer, cook in two batches. Reduce heat; simmer uncovered 20 minutes. Remove with a slotted spoon and serve immediately.

Note: Slice leftover potato dumplings and sauté in a little margarine; serve with buttered bread crumbs.

Mashed Potatoes with Fried Red Grapes

Try this recipe for a delightful Easter vegetable. If you peel the potatoes ahead of time, remember to cover them with cold water to prevent browning.

6 servings

3	cups seedless red grapes, stems removed
3/4	cup all-purpose flour
1/2	teaspoon ground cinnamon
2	egg whites, slightly beaten
2	cups dry fine whole-wheat bread crumbs
2	cups canola oil
2 3/4 to 3	pounds all-purpose white potatoes, peeled and quartered
1/4	cup (1/2 stick) margarine or butter, cut into small pieces, at room temperature
1/2	cup half-and-half or milk
1/2	teaspoon ground mace
1/2	teaspoon salt
1/4	teaspoon freshly ground white pepper

Wash but do not dry grapes. Mix flour and cinnamon on a plate. Place beaten egg whites in a shallow dish. Put crumbs in a small bowl. Tumble wet grapes in flour mixture and then gently in beaten egg whites; roll in crumbs. Place in a single layer on a plate. Refrigerate 45 minutes or more. When ready to serve, heat oil to 375 degrees in a high-sided saucepan. Carefully slide some grapes into hot oil. Cook briefly just until light brown, about 10 seconds; drain. Continue until all grapes have been cooked.

Cover potatoes with water in a large saucepan and heat to boiling; reduce heat, cook uncovered, over medium-high heat, until fork-tender, 20 to 25 minutes; drain. Return to pan; place over medium-high heat. Heat, shaking pan vigorously, until potatoes are dry, about 1 minute. Mash potatoes with a ricer, electric mixer, or potato masher. Stir in margarine, half-and-half, mace, salt, and pepper; beat until light, fluffy, and free of lumps.

To serve, spoon an individual portion of potatoes onto each plate. Make an indentation on top with the back of a spoon. Arrange grapes in the ''nest.'' If you want, mound potatoes into a serving dish and sprinkle with grapes.

Tip: To reheat mashed potatoes, either use a double boiler or melt 2 tablespoons margarine in a saucepan and stir in potatoes; heat until hot.

French Potato Pie

8 servings

Double-Crust Pastry

2¹/₂	cups all-purpose flour
¹/₂	teaspoon salt
²/₃	cup vegetable shortening
2	tablespoons margarine or butter
7 to 10	tablespoons ice water
	Flour for rolling out dough

Filling

6	medium-sized red or white potatoes, peeled and thinly sliced (about 4 cups)
1	teaspoon salt
¹/₄	teaspoon freshly ground pepper
4	ounces Gruyère cheese, thinly sliced
4	ounces lean smoked ham, thinly sliced
1	egg, slightly beaten
¹/₂	cup sour half-and-half
1	tablespoon milk
2	teaspoons chopped chives

To make pastry, mix flour and salt in a medium-sized bowl. Cut in shortening and margarine with a pastry blender, two knives, or a food processor fitted with steel blade, until mixture resembles cornmeal. Sprinkle the water, 1 tablespoon at a time, over the dough, stirring until a smooth dough is formed. Gather into a ball; divide in half. Wrap each half in plastic wrap; refrigerate at least 20 minutes.

On a lightly floured surface, roll out one half of the pastry into a 10-inch circle. Place pastry circle on an ungreased baking sheet. Toss potatoes with salt and pepper in a large bowl. Arrange about a third of potatoes on pastry, leaving a 1-inch border. Place half of the cheese and half of the ham evenly on the potatoes; repeat with another third of the potatoes, the rest of the cheese and ham, and the remaining potatoes. Heat oven to 350 degrees. Roll out the other half of the pastry into a 13-inch circle. Place the pastry over the potato mixture. Fold top edge of pastry under lower edge; flute the edge to form a 1/2-inch rim. Brush top with egg. Lightly score pastry with a fork. Make small cuts in a 5-inch circle on top of the pie, outlining a "lid" that will be removed after baking. Bake until pastry is a rich golden brown, 50 to 60 minutes. Remove and carefully lift off the pastry lid; reserve lid. Mix sour half-and-half and milk; stir in chives. Spoon into top of hot potato pie; replace lid. Serve at room temperature, cut into wedges.

Vesuvio-Style Roast Potatoes

Chicken Vesuvio is a Chicago original. Gene & Georgetti's restaurant, on Franklin Street, has been serving it for over 50 years. We created this potato dish with Vesuvio seasoning.

6 servings

4	medium-sized Russet (baking) potatoes, about 1¼ pounds, peeled
2	tablespoons olive oil
2	cloves garlic, minced
1	tablespoon chopped fresh parsley
1	teaspoon dried oregano
1	teaspoon salt
¼	teaspoon freshly ground black pepper
¼	cup dry white wine

Cut potatoes in half lengthwise, then cut each half into four long wedges. Toss potatoes with olive oil in a 9-inch by 13-inch baking pan. Combine garlic, parsley, oregano, salt, and pepper; sprinkle over potatoes. Toss to coat potatoes with spice mixture. Add wine to pan. Bake at 425 degrees until potatoes are tender, about 25 minutes. To serve, arrange potatoes in stacks.

Roasted Rosemary Potato Wedges

Serve these crusty herb-seasoned potatoes with a small portion of roasted meat, a green salad, and French bread spread with the creamy baked garlic.

6 servings

6	Russet (baking) potatoes, scrubbed and quartered lengthwise
	Olive oil for brushing potatoes
12	large cloves garlic, unpeeled
2	teaspoons chopped fresh rosemary or 1 teaspoon dried
1/2	teaspoon salt, or to taste
1/4	teaspoon freshly ground pepper
1/2	cup sliced black olives
1	loaf French bread, thinly sliced

Preheat oven to 400 degrees. Spread potatoes on a baking sheet; brush with olive oil. Sprinkle potatoes with garlic, rosemary, salt, and pepper. Bake, turning two or three times during cooking, until tender and crusty, 45 minutes to 1 hour. Spoon potatoes and garlic into a serving dish. Sprinkle with olives. Serve with French bread, spread with the softened garlic.

Potato Skins with Yogurt and Golden Caviar

6 servings

6	large Russet (baking) potatoes, unpeeled
	Canola oil for brushing potatoes
$1/2$	teaspoon ground cumin
$1/2$	teaspoon salt
$1/4$	teaspoon freshly ground pepper
6	ounces golden caviar*
3	cups plain low-fat yogurt
$3/4$	cup chopped chives

Prick potatoes about five times with a fork or sharp knife point. Place on a baking sheet; brush with oil. Bake at 400 degrees for 1 hour or until potatoes are fork-tender and skin is crisp. Remove from oven; let stand until cool enough to handle. Cut potatoes in half, horizontally. Remove potato pulp with a spoon, leaving a $1/4$- to $1/2$-inch rim attached to the skin. (Use the pulp for another dish.) Cut each potato skin half in half again, lengthwise. This can be done earlier in the day. When ready to serve, place potato skins on baking sheet; lightly brush both insides and outsides with oil. Sprinkle with mixture of cumin, salt, and pepper. Bake at 400 degrees until hot, about 10 minutes. Serve hot as an appetizer with bowls of caviar, yogurt, and chives; assemble and arrange on a tray; or serve as a first course or side dish.

*Golden caviar, made of whitefish roe, is available from Carolyn Collins Caviar, P.O. Box 662, Crystal Lake, IL 60014.

Latin American Potato Soup with Corn and Avocado

We eliminated the butter, cream, and egg yolks that were in the original recipe, substituted light cream cheese, and still have a wonderful blend of colors, textures, and flavors.

8 servings

5 to 6	medium-sized Round Red or all-purpose potatoes, peeled and diced (about 4 cups)
3	medium-sized onions, diced (about 1$\frac{1}{2}$ cups)
6	cups (48 ounces) chicken broth
1	8-ounce package Neufchâtel cheese, at room temperature
$\frac{1}{2}$	teaspoon Tabasco sauce
1	10-ounce package frozen corn
1	2-ounce jar diced pimiento, drained
2	avocadoes, peeled and sliced, for garnish

Combine potatoes, onions, and chicken broth in a large saucepan or Dutch oven. Heat to boiling; reduce heat. Cover and cook until potatoes are tender, 15 to 20 minutes. Place about 1 cup of the potato solids in a medium-sized bowl, using a slotted spoon. Mash coarsely with the spoon; stir in cheese and Tabasco sauce. Add mashed potato mixture, corn, and pimiento to the remaining potato mixture in the saucepan. Heat, but do not boil, until corn is cooked, about 3 minutes. Serve garnished with avocado slices.

Chive Potato Pancakes

This dish may also be served with yogurt or sour cream in place of the applesauce.

5 to 6 servings

4	large raw Russet (baking) potatoes, peeled, grated, and drained (about 4 cups)
1	small onion, grated
1/4	cup chopped chives
2	egg whites
1 1/2	tablespoons all-purpose flour
1/2	teaspoon salt
1/4	teaspoon baking powder
1/4	teaspoon baking soda
4	tablespoons canola oil
	Ginger Applesauce (recipe follows)

Place drained potatoes in a large mixing bowl. Stir in onion, chives, egg whites, and dry ingredients. Let stand 10 minutes. Heat oil in a large heavy skillet. Pour batter onto the hot skillet, using about a 1/4 cup batter for each pancake. Fry on both sides until cooked through and golden brown. Drain on paper toweling. Serve hot with Ginger Applesauce.

Ginger Applesauce

About 5 cups

3 1/2	pounds firm cooking apples, peeled, cored, and sliced
3/4	cup sugar
2	tablespoons ground cinnamon

1	tablespoon grated lemon zest
1/2	teaspoon grated fresh gingerroot
1/4	teaspoon ground nutmeg
1/4	cup apple juice or water

Combine apples, sugar, cinnamon, lemon zest, gingerroot, and nutmeg in a large saucepan. Stir in apple juice or water. Cover and cook over medium-low heat, stirring often, until apples have lost their shape. Taste and adjust seasonings. Add more liquid, 1/4 cup at a time, and more sugar and cinnamon, if necessary. Cool before serving.

Double-Baked Sweet Potatoes with Pomegranate and Sunflower Seeds

Prepare the potatoes early in the day and reheat them when you are ready to serve dinner.

6 servings

6	sweet potatoes, scrubbed under running water
2 to 3	tablespoons canola oil
1/4	cup (1/2 stick) margarine or butter
1/4	cup milk
3/4	teaspoon ground cinnamon
1/2	teaspoon salt
1/4	teaspoon freshly ground pepper
	Seeds of 1 small pomegranate
1/2	cup (or to taste) sunflower seeds; more for garnish

Prick potatoes about five times with a fork or sharp knife point. Place on a baking sheet; brush lightly with oil. Bake at 425 degrees until fork-tender, 45 to 55 minutes, or when they give slightly when squeezed. Remove from oven; let stand until cool enough to handle. Cut open lengthwise. Scoop out pulp into a bowl, leaving 1/4 to 1/2 inch of pulp attached to skin. Beat margarine and milk into potato pulp until smooth and margarine is melted. Stir in cinnamon, salt, pepper, pomegranate, and sunflower seeds. Spoon filling into shells; set on baking sheet. When ready to serve, bake at 375 degrees until hot, about 10 minutes. Serve with a bowl of extra sunflower seeds to sprinkle on potatoes.

Honey-Glazed Sweet Potato Chips

4 servings

2　sweet potatoes, 1¼ pounds, peeled and thinly sliced
2　tablespoons margarine or butter, melted
2　tablespoons honey
½　teaspoon ground cinnamon

Arrange potato slices in a single layer on a lightly oiled baking sheet with sides. Combine margarine and honey in a small bowl; drizzle over the potatoes. Sprinkle with cinnamon. Broil 5 minutes; turn and broil just until tender, about 2 minutes.

Potato and Carrot Tzimmes

Each of Barbara's cookbooks has at least one recipe that she remembers fondly from her mother's kitchen. As the family had a central European background, potatoes played a strong part in their cuisine. This recipe was prepared only for holidays. Tzimmes means "a fuss about nothing" or "a stew"—in this case, an aromatic beef stew with carrots and sweet potatoes, sweetened with prunes and/or apricots and raisins. A tzimmes can be a main dish, served just with a salad, or it can be a side dish. It's even better reheated as a leftover. Enjoy this slow-cooked vegetable-dense stew!

8-plus servings

1½	pounds lean chuck or beef brisket, cut into small pieces
1	pound carrots, sliced
4	sweet potatoes, peeled and sliced
3	all-purpose red potatoes, peeled and sliced
2	cups pitted prunes or apricots, or a combination
1	cup golden raisins
¼	cup firmly packed dark brown sugar *or*
¼	cup honey
3	tablespoons freshly squeezed lemon juice
	Salt
	Freshly ground pepper
¼	cup water

Place meat in a large heavy pot or Dutch oven. Add carrots, sweet potatoes, red potatoes, prunes, and raisins. Sprinkle with remaining ingredients; season with salt and pepper to taste. Cook covered over medium-low heat for 10 minutes. Add ¼ cup water. Continue cooking, stirring once or twice, for 45 minutes. Add more water, up to 1 cup, if the tzimmes seems dry. Cook covered in a 325-degree oven until the vegetables are very soft and the meat is tender, about 2 hours.

For special occasions, Barbara's mother spread potato pancake batter on top of the tzimmes and cooked it uncovered for the last 20 to 30 minutes of baking. The family would all wait expectantly as Mother spooned through the steaming crusty potato topping and served it together with the tzimmes.

Warm Grilled Catfish Salad with Sweet Potatoes and Greens

It used to be that we ate bacon with eggs for breakfast. Now, we use it sparingly to flavor dishes that are otherwise low in fat. If you'd rather omit the bacon, brush the fish fillets with oil before broiling them.

4 servings

2	sweet potatoes, about 1 pound, peeled and cut into 1/2-inch cubes
1/2	cup pecan halves
4	tablespoons olive oil, divided
1/2	teaspoon chili powder
2	tablespoons balsamic vinegar
1	teaspoon salt
	Freshly ground pepper
3	scallions with tender green tops, sliced
1 1/2	pounds catfish fillets
4	slices hickory-smoked bacon, cut in half
1	pound fresh spinach
2	tablespoons mayonnaise
4 to 5 drops	(or to taste) Tabasco sauce

Toss sweet potatoes and pecans with 1 tablespoon of the olive oil and the chili powder in a medium-sized baking pan. Bake at 450 degrees for 15 minutes, stirring once. Whisk remaining oil, vinegar, salt, and pepper to taste in a small bowl; add scallions. Remove potatoes and pecans from the oven; stir in oil-and-vinegar mixture. Reserve. Cut catfish into eight rectangular pieces, folding narrow ends under to form neat bundles. Wrap a half slice of bacon around each piece of fish; fasten with foodpicks. Broil 3 minutes; turn and broil until fish flakes easily when prodded with a fork, 2 to 3 minutes more. Remove and reserve.

While fish is cooking, wash spinach. Place in a Dutch oven with just the water that clings to the leaves. Cover and steam until wilted; drain thoroughly. Arrange spinach in a ring on four dinner plates. Arrange sweet potatoes and pecans on spinach. Place two pieces of fish in center of ring. Mix mayonnaise and hot sauce; spoon one heaping teaspoon mayonnaise on top of each serving.

Skillet Potato Salad with Wild Mushrooms and Lemon Dressing

4 servings

3   tablespoons margarine or butter, divided

1   cup, about 4 ounces, variety mushrooms (shiitake, enoki, etc.), cleaned, trimmed, and sliced lengthwise

1   cup chicken broth

1   cup, about 8-ounces, new red potatoes, peeled and sliced 1/8 inch thick

4   cups mixed greens, cleaned

1   tablespoon freshly squeezed lemon juice

    Freshly ground pepper

Heat 1 tablespoon of the margarine in an 8-inch skillet. Sauté mushrooms over medium heat until tender, about 5 minutes; remove and reserve. Add chicken broth to skillet; heat to boiling. Add potatoes and reduce heat. Cover and cook just until tender, 5 to 6 minutes. Arrange greens equally on four serving plates. With slotted spoon, remove potatoes and arrange on one side of greens; arrange mushrooms next to the potatoes. Stir remaining margarine into chicken broth in skillet until margarine is melted and the broth is slightly thickened. Stir in lemon juice; pour 3 to 4 tablespoons of the broth over each salad. Top with a grinding of fresh pepper.

Escargot-Stuffed Potatoes

Carolyn Buster, chef/owner of The Cottage restaurant in Calumet City, Illinois, pairs tiny new potatoes with escargot in an elegant appetizer or first-course dish.

8 servings (3 potatoes/serving)

24	tiny new red or white potatoes, cooked just until tender
24	whole escargot (more or less depending on size)
1/2	cup (1 stick) butter
3	cloves garlic, minced
1 1/2	teaspoons salt
1	tablespoon finely minced shallots
1	teaspoon freshly ground black pepper
	Worcestershire sauce
	Tabasco sauce
2	tablespoons chopped fresh parsley

Drain potatoes; let stand until cool enough to handle. Trim the bottoms flat so that they will stand. Slice off the top, about one-third down. Remove the centers from potatoes with a small melon baller, leaving a thin potato shell. Place one escargot in each potato. Cream butter in a food processor. Mash garlic with the salt; add to butter with the shallots, pepper, and Worcestershire and Tabasco sauce to taste. Add chopped parsley and process just long enough to incorporate parsley. Pipe butter mixture over escargot in potatoes, mounding slightly. Refrigerate. When ready to serve, bake in a preheated 375-degree oven until hot and bubbly.

Old Recipe for Potato Bread

While we were working on this book, Barbara and Jerry Grunes went to Cincinnati, and on their way home, they stopped at a roadside antique shop. Barbara bought an old cookbook, published in 1915. When she was leafing through the book, a yellowed, much-handled piece of paper fell out with this recipe written on it. Whoever wrote that recipe, we thank you for the treasure. It works perfectly and is delicious.

2 loaves

1	¹/₄-ounce package active dry yeast
²/₃	cup sugar, divided
1¹/₄	cup warm water (105° to 115°F), divided
7¹/₂	cups all-purpose flour, divided
²/₃	cup shortening or margarine
2	eggs, beaten
1	cup cooled mashed potatoes
1	teaspoon salt
¹/₄	teaspoon grated fresh nutmeg *or* ¹/₈ teaspoon ground nutmeg

Dissolve yeast and 2 teaspoons of the sugar in ¹/₂ cup of the warm water in a medium-sized bowl until foamy. Stir in ³/₄ cup of the flour; let stand in a warm draft-free place until mixture becomes spongy, about 10 minutes. Meanwhile, cream shortening and remaining sugar in a large bowl with an electric mixer. Beat in eggs, yeast mixture, mashed potatoes, salt, and nutmeg on low speed. Add remaining flour alternately with the remaining ³/₄ cup water using a dough hook or kneading by hand when too stiff for the mixer. Place dough in a large oiled bowl; turn to grease evenly. Cover with plastic wrap and a sheet of aluminum foil. Let stand in a warm draft-free place until dough has doubled, about 2 hours. Punch down dough. Divide dough in half. Place in greased loaf pans. Let rise until doubled, about 1 hour. Preheat oven to 350 degrees. Bake until bread loaves sound hollow when tapped and tops are golden, about 45 minutes. Let cool 5 minutes; remove from pans and let cool completely on a wire rack.

Cinnamon (Potato) Doughnut Holes

24 to 30 doughnut holes

2¹/₂	cups sugar, divided
3	tablespoons margarine or butter
2	eggs, slightly beaten
¹/₂	cup milk
1	cup all-purpose flour
4	teaspoons baking powder
1	teaspoon plus 4 tablespoons ground cinnamon, divided
¹/₂	teaspoon salt
1	cup cooled mashed potatoes
	Flour for rolling out dough
2	cups canola oil
¹/₄	teaspoon ground mace

Beat 1¹/₂ cups of the sugar and the margarine in a large bowl with an electric mixer until combined. Add eggs; beat until light and lemon colored. Gradually add milk. Beat in flour, baking powder, 1 teaspoon of the cinnamon, salt, and mashed potatoes. Roll out dough on a lightly floured board to ³/₄ inch thick. Cut with a doughnut hole (one-inch round) cutter, or form into walnut-sized balls. Heat oil to 375 degrees in a medium-sized saucepan with high sides. Cook holes, about six at a time, until puffy and golden brown on all sides. Remove with a slotted spoon and drain on paper toweling. Combine remaining 4 tablespoons cinnamon and the mace; roll hot doughnut holes in this mixture.

Southwest Yam Muffins

This and the next recipe are two delicious ways to make muffins using mashed sweet potatoes.

12 muffins

2	cups all-purpose flour
3	tablespoons minced dried onion
2	teaspoons cumin seeds
2	teaspoons baking powder
1/2	teaspoon baking soda
1/2	teaspoon salt
1/4	teaspoon freshly ground black pepper
1	egg plus 2 egg whites
3/4	cups packed brown sugar
1 1/3	cups cooked, peeled, and mashed sweet potatoes
1/2	cup (1 stick) margarine or butter, at room temperature
1/2	cup milk
3/4	cup chopped pecans

Heat oven to 400 degrees. Line a muffin tin with paper liners. Mix flour, dried onion, cumin, baking powder, baking soda, salt, and pepper in a small bowl; reserve. Beat egg, egg whites, and brown sugar in a large bowl with an electric mixer until thick. Beat in sweet potatoes and margarine. With a spatula or wooden spoon, stir in milk, flour mixture, and pecans; do not overmix. Fill muffin cups three-quarters full. Bake until muffins test done, about 20 minutes. Remove from pan and cool on a rack. Serve warm.

Sweet Potato Muffins with Dried Cherries

12 muffins

2	cups all-purpose flour
2	teaspoons baking powder
1	teaspoon ground cinnamon
1/2	teaspoon baking soda
1/2	teaspoon salt
1/2	teaspoon ground mace
1	cup dried cherries
1	egg plus 2 egg whites
1/3	cup granulated sugar
1/3	cup packed light brown sugar
1 1/3	cups cooked, peeled, and mashed sweet potatoes
1/2	cup (1 stick) margarine or butter, melted
1/2	cup milk

Heat oven to 400 degrees. Line a muffin tin with paper liners. Combine flour, baking powder, cinnamon, baking soda, salt, mace, and cherries in a small bowl; reserve. Beat egg, egg whites, and sugars in a large bowl with an electric mixer until thick. Beat in sweet potatoes and margarine. With a spatula or wooden spoon, stir in milk and reserved flour mixture just until combined; do not overmix. Fill muffin cups three-quarters full. Bake until muffins test done, about 20 minutes. Remove from pan and cool on a rack. Serve warm.

Note: If dried cherries are not available, substitute raisins or currants. If you like a sweeter muffin, sprinkle with a mixture of cinnamon and sugar before baking. A drained, mashed 14-ounce can of sweet potatoes (yams) can be substituted for the freshly cooked sweet potatoes.

Old Fashioned Potato Fondant

Here's a very old-fashioned candy that used to be a favorite at holiday bake sales.

6 dozen slices

$1/2$	cup cold cooked, unpeeled, and mashed all-purpose white potatoes
$1/2$	teaspoon vanilla
$1/4$	teaspoon salt
4 to $4^1/2$	cups sifted confectioners' sugar, divided
1	cup smooth peanut butter, divided

Mix potatoes, vanilla, salt, and 2 cups of the confectioners' sugar in a large bowl. Gradually stir in enough of the remaining sugar to form a stiff dough that leaves the side of the bowl and is no longer sticky. Divide mixture in half. Pat or roll each portion to a 10-inch by 7-inch rectangle on a surface liberally sprinkled with confectioners' sugar. Spread $1/2$ cup of the peanut butter over each rectangle to within $1/2$ inch of the edge. Roll up, beginning with the wide edge. Wrap rolls in waxed paper or plastic wrap. Refrigerate at least 2 hours. Cut into $1/4$-inch slices. Store in refrigerator up to 1 week.

Sweet Potato Nut Bread

This orange-scented nut bread is a wonderful addition to a holiday meal bread basket. But don't limit it to special occasions. It's delicious for breakfast, toasted with a light topping of red currant jelly. Or use it for an innovative turkey sandwich with curry-spiked mayonnaise.

1 loaf

1³/₄	cups all-purpose flour
2	teaspoons baking powder
³/₄	teaspoons ground cinnamon
¹/₂	teaspoon baking soda
¹/₂	teaspoon salt
¹/₂	teaspoon ground nutmeg
¹/₄	teaspoon ground cloves
	Grated zest of 1 orange
³/₄	cups chopped walnuts
¹/₂	cup dried currants
1	egg plus 2 egg whites
¹/₃	cup granulated sugar
¹/₃	cup packed light brown sugar
1¹/₃	cups cooked, peeled, and pureed sweet potatoes
¹/₂	cup (1 stick) margarine or butter, melted
¹/₂	cup buttermilk

Heat oven to 350 degrees. Grease a 9-inch by 5-inch loaf pan. Combine flour, baking powder, cinnamon, baking soda, salt, nutmeg, cloves, orange zest, walnuts, and currants in a medium-sized bowl; reserve. Beat egg, egg whites, and sugars in a large mixing bowl with an electric mixer until thick. Add sweet potatoes, margarine, and buttermilk. Gradually beat in the reserved flour mixture. Pour batter into prepared pan. Bake until a tester comes out dry when inserted in center, about 55 minutes. Remove from oven and let stand 5 minutes. Remove bread from pan and let cool on a rack. Serve warm or cold.

Sweet Potato Pie with Ginger Meringue

6 to 8 servings

Single Crust Pastry

- 1¼ cups all-purpose flour
- ¼ teaspoon salt
- ⅓ cup solid vegetable shortening
- 2 tablespoons margarine or butter
- 6 tablespoons ice water (approximately)
- Flour for rolling out dough

Filling

- 2 eggs plus 2 egg whites, slightly beaten
- ¾ cup packed light brown sugar
- 2 tablespoons margarine or butter, at room temperature
- 2½ cups warm, cooked, peeled, and pureed sweet potatoes
- ¾ cup milk
- 2 tablespoons grated orange zest
- 1 teaspoon grated fresh gingerroot
- 1½ teaspoons ground cinnamon
- ¼ teaspoon ground mace
- ¼ teaspoon ground allspice

Ginger Meringue

5	egg whites, at room temperature
1/2	cup granulated sugar
1/4	teaspoon cream of tartar
1/4	cup (or to taste) finely minced candied ginger

To make pie crust, mix flour and salt in a medium-sized bowl. Cut in shortening and margarine with a pastry blender, two knives, or a food processor fitted with steel blade, until mixture resembles cornmeal. Sprinkle the water, 1 tablespoon at a time, over the dough, stirring until a smooth dough is formed; gather into a ball. Wrap in plastic wrap. Refrigerate at least 20 minutes. Roll out dough on a lightly floured surface or pastry cloth. Fit into a 9-inch pie pan or dish.

Heat oven to 400 degrees. Mix eggs, egg whites, brown sugar, and margarine in a medium-sized bowl. Beat in sweet potatoes and milk. Stir in remaining ingredients. Mound filling into unbaked pie shell; bake 15 minutes. Reduce heat to 350 degrees. Bake until filling is slightly firm to the touch, 25 to 30 minutes.

While pie is baking, make Ginger Meringue: Beat egg whites in a large bowl with an electric mixer until soft peaks form. Sprinkle granulated sugar and cream of tartar over egg whites; beat until sugar is incorporated and egg whites are stiff. Stir in candied ginger. Remove pie from oven; spread meringue over pie, being careful not to leave spaces around the edges. Continue baking at 350 degrees until meringue is golden brown, about 10 minutes.

Mashed Potato Chocolate Cake

8 servings

Cake

1	cup (2 sticks) margarine or butter, at room temperature
2	cups sugar
1	cup warm cooked, peeled, and mashed all-purpose white or red potatoes
1/2	cup unsweetened cocoa
1	extra large egg plus 2 egg whites
2 1/2	cups cake flour
1	teaspoon baking soda
1	teaspoon baking powder
1/2	teaspoon salt
3/4	cup buttermilk
1	teaspoon vanilla

Frosting

1/2	cup (1 stick) butter (or mixture of butter and margarine), at room temperature
3	cups sifted confectioners' sugar
1/2	cold cooked, peeled, and mashed all-purpose red or white potatoes
1/2	cup unsweetened cocoa
2	tablespoons milk (or more to achieve desired consistency)
1	teaspoon vanilla

Grease and flour a 9-inch by 5-inch loaf pan. Preheat oven to 350 degrees. Cream butter and sugar in a large bowl with an electric mixer. Mix in potatoes and cocoa; add eggs. Mix flour, baking soda, baking powder, and salt; add alternately with buttermilk. Stir in vanilla. Pour into prepared pan. Bake until a tester comes out clean, about 1 hour and 20 minutes. Let cool 5 minutes. Remove from pan and cool completely on a wire rack. If you wish, you can split this dense cake and spread frosting between the layers.

To make frosting, beat butter in a large bowl with an electric mixer or food processor until light and fluffy. Gradually add confectioners' sugar, beating until light. Beat in mashed potatoes, cocoa, milk if necessary, and vanilla. Spread on cooled cake. Also works well as a layer cake. Use two 9$^1/_2$-inch baking pans and bake 25 minutes or until done; cake will spring back when prodded.

THREE

ONIONS, LEEKS, SHALLOTS, AND GARLIC

Onions and their culinary relations belong to the noble *allium* or lily family that includes the tulip, hyacinth, and lily-of-the-valley. Since prehistoric times, onions and garlic have been venerated for their spiritual, medicinal, and culinary qualities. For the world's first great civilizations in Sumer and Egypt, the onion was a symbol of eternity. In ancient Rome, laborers were given garlic for strength, and soldiers ate it for courage. The Greeks fed garlic to prisoners to cleanse their souls. The Bible records that the children of Israel longed for onions, leeks, and garlic to jazz up the manna they lived on during their wanderings in the desert (Numbers 11:5,6).

What greater tribute can be given to a root vegetable than to name the great hub of the heartland, Chicago, in its honor. Originally, the banks of the rivers in that area were covered with what regional Native Americans called *Che-cau-gou*, a type of wild onion. The onions still exist but are hard to grow since they don't transplant easily.

From early times, onions have been used for medicinal purposes: poor eyesight, dog and snake bites, "stings of venomous worms," stomach problems, baldness, diabetes, rheumatism, poor complexion, fever, laryngitis, warts, earache, and fever. A 14th-century Icelandic manuscript advises rubbing a mixture of onion juice and chicken fat on shoes that cause blisters. In not so ancient times, one of your authors was given garlic sandwiches to remedy a childhood case of pinworms. It must have worked because she doesn't remember having to endure very many treatments.

Curiously, there is a renewed interest in the medicinal value of onions and garlic. A number of studies have been done and are continuing to explore the antibiotic and antioxidant properties of onions and garlic. There is considerable evidence that garlic works like aspirin to reduce the clotting caused by LDL, the "bad" cholesterol in blood. In one study, 20 patients with high cholesterol levels who ate a raw white onion every day increased their heart-healthy HDL cholesterol by 30 percent. Mild red onions and all cooked onions had little or no effect.

In animal studies, raw garlic has inhibited colon, stomach, and breast cancer and killed vaginal yeast infections. Antibiotic effects of garlic and onions are greatly reduced when heated, but anticancer properties are unaltered. Different varieties and preparations of onions and garlic have unique protective qualities, so eat them all: raw, steamed, sautéed, baked, grilled—and see the doctor if you have any symptoms of heart disease, cancer, or infections.

Onions and their siblings are all low in sodium, fat, and calories (unless they're prepared with undue amounts of cream sauce or deep-fried batter). We like to think of garlic as a ''fat substitute.'' We use roasted garlic instead of butter on bread and vegetables and to give flavor to poached or grilled fish and poultry. Onions and garlic do not rate high on the list of nutrient-dense foods, but their potential healing powers earn them a prominent place in a healthful diet.

Over the years, newspapers and magazines have printed numerous tips about how to prepare onions without tears. We haven't tested this compendium of suggestions since we enjoy a good oniony cry, but they might work for you.

- Use a sharp knife. Dull knives bruise cells and release more fumes.
- Peel onions under running water.
- Rinse onions in boiling water. (That does make them easier to peel.)
- Hold a piece of bread in your mouth.
- Chill onions in the freezer for 20 to 30 minutes before peeling.
- Wear goggles.

A good rule to remember about both garlic and onions is that the longer you cook them, the milder they become. Also, like peppercorns, the more you do to garlic—mash, smash, chop, press—the stronger its flavor. We often blanch strong-flavored onions and garlic (a quick microwaving will do) rather than adding them raw to dishes where they will not be cooked. Put grilled red onions or leeks in a sandwich and elevate it from ordinary to sublime fare.

When you go into the supermarket these days, you'll find three or four kinds of onions (maybe more) and several types of garlic. The following charts will tell you how to select and store dry onions, scallions and leeks, and garlic.

Onion and Garlic Selection and Storage

Dry Onions

After harvesting, onions are cured. The neck of the onion closes, which seals out moisture-producing decay. Onions harvested in late summer are fully cured to last through the winter. A fully cured onion has skin dry enough to rustle. Choose firm onions with no soft spots (especially by the neck), no black powder under the skin, or sprouting. The skins should be clean and crisp. Store in a cool, dry place with good circulation. A strong-tasting onion will keep longer than a milder onion, but an onion that smells strong may have begun to rot. Never store onions with potatoes; they will absorb moisture from potatoes and decay rapidly. Refrigerating onions will prolong their shelf life, but they will pass along their flavor to butter, eggs, and milk. A cut onion should be wrapped tightly in plastic wrap and refrigerated and used in 2 to 3 days. A carbon steel knife will discolor an onion.

DRY ONION GUIDE

Type	Description	Use	Storage/Preparation
Bermuda; includes Granex-Grano varieties; also called Short Day	Named for their place of origin, these onions are large and flat with ivory or yellow skins. About 2–3 per pound. Usually sold in bulk. Most readily available from March to June.	Mild and sweet; use when raw onions are called for.	Store 1–2 weeks.
Spanish; also called Long Day	Often confused with Bermudas as they are large and tan. They average $1/2$ pound each. Available August through May.	Mild and sweet, but better cooked than raw. Good stuffed, baked, grilled, fried.	Store 1–2 weeks.
Red or Italian; also called Creole	Dark purple skins; rings of white flesh with red outer layer. Vary in size. Available year-round.	Strong flavor, though there are regional differences. Often used in antipasti and salads. Good grilled.	Store 1–2 weeks.
Yellow or Golden Globe; also called Late Crop	Round, golden onions with dry skin. Available, often in 3-pound mesh bags, year-round.	Strong flavor when raw but mild when cooked. Size has nothing to do with flavor.	Store up to 1 month.
Summer specialties: Walla Walla, Maui, Vidalia	Medium to large in size; usually yellow skins. Often billed as "sweet enough to eat like an apple." Available in summer months.	Sweet, with softer texture than other onions. Good raw or grilled.	Very short shelf life—no more than 1 to 2 weeks. To order Vidalia onions, call 1-800-843-2542.

DRY ONION GUIDE (concluded)

Type	Description	Use	Storage/Preparation
White, including boiling, pearl, pickling, cocktail onions	Mild, small-sized, firm onions	Boiling onions are about the size of a walnut (18–24/pound); used in stews and for creaming. Other varieties are even smaller.	Store 3 to 4 weeks. To remove skins, cover with boiling water; let stand 3 minutes. Drain; cover with cold water. Remove skins. Make an X in the bottom to keep them from coming apart during cooking.
Shallots	Shallots are shaped like cloves of garlic. They come from third-year onions. The first year provides an onion set; the second a mature onion; the third a shallot offshoot, like a dividing tulip bulb. Small quantities are sold in baskets or bags.	Mild in flavor and easier to digest than mature onions.	Short shelf life—3 weeks maximum at room temperature. Store in refrigerator loosely wrapped in paper toweling or (peeled) in olive oil in covered container.

Scallions and Leeks

These perishable, fresh onions should be kept in the refrigerator. The green ends should be crisp and brightly colored. The white ends should not be slimy or coming apart.

FRESH ONION GUIDE

Type	Description	Use	Storage/Preparation
Scallions, also called green onions, spring onions	A round bulbous end with white stems 2 to 3 inches long. Sold in bunches of 5–6 stalks.	White part is milder than green. Whites and tender green tops are eaten raw or cooked. Blanched whole greens make nice garnish. Can be substituted for leeks.	Wipe with wet paper towel; refrigerate in plastic bag up to 2 weeks.
Knob onions	Mature scallions with large bulb. Usually sold in bunches of 4–5 stalks.	Use bulbs as you would a dry white onion.	Store as you would a scallion.
Leeks	A tall straight thick white base and dark green leaves. One bunch (3–4) = 1 pound.	Flavor distinct from other onions. Rarely used raw; parboil 8 to 10 minutes for salads; often used in soup; excellent grilled.	Trim top; cut lengthwise to $1^1/_2$ inches from base. Spread layers apart and wash well to remove grit. Trim green part to 2 inches.

Garlic

A *head* of garlic is a cluster of *cloves*. The head is covered with a thin skin; each clove is encased in another skin. One of the best ways to remove the skin from the cloves is to mash the clove with the flat side of a knife—the skin will come right off. Crushed or chopped garlic is about three times as potent as whole garlic cloves. Always remove the skin of the garlic before eating it. Store away from potatoes and onions.

GARLIC GUIDE

Type	Description	Use	Storage/Preparation
Creole	Usually sold in bulk. Heads are about the size of a tangerine. Heads are covered with white papery skin.	Milder flavor than Italian type.	Good all-purpose garlic. When recipe calls for a clove, use amount equal to end of your little finger.
Elephant; also known as Tahiti garlic	Large individual cloves are dark pink or red.	Milder and sweeter than other varieties.	Store in a dry, well-ventilated place up to 1 month.
Italian	Small heads. Usually sold 2 to a box. Pinkish in color.	Strongest flavor.	Store in a dark place with good circulation. Best variety for storage—up to 2 months. Can be chopped and stored in covered jar in refrigerator, covered with oil, up to 3 months.

Oven-Baked Onion Soup

If you use canned beef broth instead of homemade, adjust the salt to taste. For a richer soup, brown a ¹/₂ pound lean ground beef with the onions. Food lore has it that onion soup was created for King Louis XIV of France.

6 servings

4	tablespoons (¹/₂ stick) margarine or butter
6	cups thinly sliced yellow onions
2	tablespoons all-purpose flour
1¹/₄ to 1¹/₂	quarts beef broth
¹/₂	cup dry white wine
¹/₂	teaspoon salt
¹/₂	teaspoon freshly ground pepper
6	slices French bread, toasted
6	slices Swiss cheese
¹/₂	cup freshly grated Parmesan cheese

Melt margarine in a large heavy Dutch oven or soup pot. Sauté onions over medium-low heat, stirring occasionally until light brown. Sprinkle flour over the onions; stir into onions. Stir in beef broth, wine, salt, and pepper. Heat to boiling. Reduce heat; simmer uncovered 10 minutes. Place a slice of bread in each of six small ovenproof soup dishes. Ladle soup over bread. Place one slice Swiss cheese in each soup dish; sprinkle with Parmesan cheese. Bake at 375 degrees until cheese has melted, about 5 minutes. Serve hot.

Fried Onions in a Flower Pot

Molded fried onions are an unusual appetizer. They are also fun to serve as an edible centerpiece along with hamburgers, steak, or grilled chicken.

6 servings

1	8-inch new clay flower pot (or loaf pan)
1	egg
1¹/₂	cups all-purpose flour
¹/₂	teaspoon baking soda
¹/₂	teaspoon salt
1³/₄	cups buttermilk
5	large Spanish or yellow onions, peeled, and sliced into rings ¹/₂ to 1 inch thick
	Canola oil for frying
	Salt for sprinkling

Rinse flower pot; drain. Beat egg in a medium-sized bowl; add flour, baking soda, and salt. Gradually add buttermilk. Let batter stand at room temperature 20 minutes. Separate onions into rings. Heat oil to 375 degrees in a wok or skillet with high sides; heat oven to 375 degrees. Coat onion rings with batter; cook in hot oil, a few at a time, until golden. Drain on paper toweling. Sprinkle with salt. Repeat until all onions are cooked. Stack the onion rings in the flower pot. Pack down slightly. Bake for 15 minutes. Unmold and serve hot. Let guests pull off onions as desired.

Flat Onion Bread

One 10-inch round bread

³/₄	cup warm water (105° to 115°F)
1	¹/₄-ounce package active dry yeast
1	teaspoon honey
2¹/₂	cups all-purpose flour
4	tablespoons canola oil, divided
1	egg, slightly beaten
1	teaspoon salt, divided
2	cups chopped yellow onions
1¹/₂	tablespoons poppy seeds
¹/₄	teaspoon celery seed
¹/₈	teaspoon freshly ground pepper
	Flour for rolling out dough
1	egg white, slightly beaten
	Plain nonfat yogurt (optional)

Combine water, yeast, and honey in a small bowl. Let stand until it bubbles, 5 to 8 minutes. Place flour in a deep bowl or large bowl of electric mixer. Make well in center and add yeast mixture, 1 tablespoon of the oil, egg, and ¹/₂ teaspoon of the salt. If using electric mixer, mix on lowest setting with dough hook. Gradually increase speed to high; continue mixing until dough is mixed but still sticky, 3 to 4 minutes. Add flour, if necessary, 1 tablespoon at a time, until dough is moderately soft. Place dough on a lightly floured surface; knead until smooth. Place dough in a lightly greased bowl; turn once to grease all sides. Cover and let stand in a warm draft-free place until doubled, about 1 hour.

While dough is rising, prepare onions. Heat the remaining 3 tablespoons oil in a small skillet over medium heat. Cook onions, stirring occasionally, until golden brown, 5 to 6 minutes. Stir in poppy seeds, the remaining $1/2$ teaspoon salt, celery seed, and the pepper. Reserve.

Roll out dough into a circle or rectangle on a lightly floured board to $1/4$-inch thickness. Brush with egg white. Spoon onion mixture evenly over the dough, leaving a $3/4$-inch rim. Prick dough several times with a fork so that it will stay flat during baking. Place on greased baking sheet. Bake at 375 degrees until light brown around the edges and cooked through, 30 to 35 minutes. Best served warm with dollops of yogurt.

Welch Grandma's Pickled Onions

These tiny pickled onions are good with shelled toasted walnuts as an appetizer or served as an accompaniment to chicken or meat dishes.

6 to 8 servings

2	quarts water
2	tablespoons noniodized salt
2	pounds pearl or small white onions, peeled*
1	pint (2 cups) red wine vinegar
1/2	cup sugar
3	tablespoons pickling spice
2	bay leaves

Heat water and salt to boiling; remove from heat and let stand until cool. Pour cooled salted water over onions in a large deep bowl. Cover and refrigerate overnight. Drain and rinse. Put onions in a sterilized jar or bowl; reserve. Combine remaining ingredients in a medium-sized saucepan. Heat to boiling over medium heat; pour over onions. Cover and refrigerate three days before serving.

*See directions for peeling in the chart presented earlier in this chapter.

Mediterranean Onion Salad

This unusual sweet/sour salad goes well with Greek-style lamb or chicken.

6 to 8 servings

1	cup water
1	cup dry white wine
1/4	cup olive oil
2	cloves garlic, minced
1	teaspoon mustard seeds
1	teaspoon salt
4	whole cloves
3	pounds, about 48, small white boiling onions, peeled*
1	cup golden raisins
2	teaspoons sugar
2	tablespoons snipped Italian (flat-leaf) parsley
	Freshly ground black pepper

Combine water, wine, olive oil, garlic, mustard seeds, and salt in a medium-sized saucepan. Stick the whole cloves into one of the onions; add all of the onions to the saucepan. Heat to boiling; reduce heat. Cover and simmer over medium heat until onions are just tender, about 10 minutes. Stir in raisins and sugar; continue to cook 5 minutes. Drain the onions; discard onion with the cloves. Stir in parsley. Cover and refrigerate at least 2 hours. Serve at room temperature with a grinding of fresh pepper.

*See directions for peeling in the chart presented earlier in this chapter.

Wild Onion Cornbread Stuffing

The sweet, mild taste of wild onions resembles young leeks, which can be used as a substitute. Take care not to confuse wild onions with wild leeks. Wild leeks, called "ramps," have a very strong flavor and odor. Anne's husband, Bruce, once brought his foodie wife a bag of ramps from North Carolina where he had been on business. He stowed them in the airplane's overhead bin. At the end of the flight, he opened the bin and the pungent odor of the ramps filled the plane. Those closest to him began looking for the nearest emergency exit!

Enough for 1 roasting chicken

3	cups Wild Onion Cornbread (recipe follows)
3	tablespoons canola oil
1	medium-sized onion, minced
1	carrot, peeled and grated
1/3	cup minced fresh parsley
1/2	teaspoon dried sage
1/2	teaspoon dried thyme
	Roasting chicken (3 to 5 pounds)
	Soft margarine or butter
	Salt
	Freshly ground pepper

Crumble cornbread into a medium-sized bowl; reserve. Heat oil in a medium-sized skillet over medium heat. Cook onion and carrot 5 minutes, stirring occasionally. Stir onion and carrot and remaining ingredients into cornbread. Instead of stuffing the cavity of the chicken, loosen skin from around the breast area of the chicken. Spoon stuffing under the skin. Rub chicken with soft margarine or butter, and season with salt and pepper.

Roast at 375 degrees for 1 hour or until thermometer registers 170 degrees in breast and 185 degrees in thigh.

Wild Onion Cornbread

One 9-inch square

1	cup all-purpose flour
3/4	cup yellow or white cornmeal
3	tablespoons sugar
2	teaspoons baking powder
1/2	teaspoon baking soda
1/2	teaspoon salt
1/4	teaspoon freshly ground pepper
1/2	cup chopped wild onions or young leeks, white part only
1	cup nonfat plain yogurt
1	egg
2	tablespoons margarine or butter, melted and cooled

Preheat oven to 400 degrees. Combine flour, cornmeal, sugar, baking powder, baking soda, salt, and pepper in a medium-sized bowl. Stir in wild onions. Make a well in the center. Stir in remaining ingredients, just until combined. Do not overstir. Pour into a greased 9-inch square pan. Bake until cornbread tests done when a tester inserted in the center comes out dry, 20 to 25 minutes. Cool 5 minutes. Remove from pan and cut into serving pieces or reserve for stuffing.

Baked Vidalia Onions with Shallots and Goat Cheese

Vidalia onions are raised primarily in Georgia. The climate and soil pro-duce a wonderful, sweet, easily digested onion.

6 servings

6	medium-large Vidalia onions, unpeeled and root removed
1	cup chicken broth
5	tablespoons canola oil, divided
1/2	teaspoon salt
1/2	teaspoon dried basil
	Freshly ground pepper
4	ounces goat cheese
6	large shallots, with skins

Arrange onions in a baking dish just large enough to hold them. Pour chicken broth into the dish. Mix 3 tablespoons of the oil, salt, and basil in a small dish. Brush onions with oil mixture. Bake at 325 degrees until onions are golden brown and slightly soft when touched, about 1 hour and 20 minutes. Coat shallots with remaining oil; place in a small ovenproof dish or baking pan. Bake along with onions until tender, about 30 minutes.

Set one onion on each serving plate. Make two horizontal cuts across onion, about three layers deep. Pull back the layers, exposing the remaining onion. Mix goat cheese with pepper. Spoon into the center of onions. Serve one shallot with each onion. Guests will cut open the shallot and spread the soft flesh over the onion and/or cheese. You might want to serve the onions on a bed of chopped parsley or cilantro.

Glazed Shallots

This dish takes us back to the days of grand meals in great manor houses. If you aren't up to roasted pheasant or venison, serve Glazed Shallots with grilled meat or poultry to make an everyday meal an elegant repast.

6 servings

18	medium to large shallots, trimmed and peeled
2¹/₂	tablespoons melted margarine or butter, divided
3	tablespoons sugar, divided
1	tablespoon grated lemon zest
5	tablespoons tarragon vinegar
2	tablespoons dry white wine

Place shallots in a shallow baking dish or pie plate. Brush with 1¹/₂ tablespoons of the melted margarine. Combine 2 tablespoons of the sugar, lemon zest, vinegar, and wine in a small bowl; drizzle over shallots, then stir to coat them with the mixture. Bake uncovered at 350 degrees for 1 hour. Combine remaining 1 tablespoon melted margarine and 1 tablespoon sugar; sprinkle over shallots. Continue baking until liquid has evaporated and shallots are soft and glazed but still retain their shape, about 30 minutes.

Caramelized Red Onions

This wonderful condiment can be used in many ways. Try it with mashed, boned, smoked fish mixed in equal parts with creamed cottage cheese. Or serve a piece of grilled fish on a bed of caramelized onions. How about a sandwich of leftover roast pork and Caramelized Red Onions on dark rye?

6 to 8 servings

3	tablespoons canola oil
3	tablespoons margarine or butter
2	large cloves garlic, minced
3	large red onions, thinly sliced
$1/3$	cup firmly packed light brown sugar
$1/2$	teaspoon freshly ground pepper
$1/2$	teaspoon dried tarragon
$1/2$	teaspoon grated fresh gingerroot
$1/4$	teaspoon salt

Heat oil and margarine in a large skillet over medium-low heat. Cook garlic and onions, stirring occasionally, until soft but not brown, about 5 minutes. Stir in the brown sugar, pepper, tarragon, gingerroot, and salt. Continue cooking, stirring occasionally, until onions are glazed and soft, about 4 minutes. Serve warm.

Minted Leek and Potato Soup

On a steamy summer day, serve this soup cold in a glass bowl, garnished with fresh mint leaves. Pass a small decanter of additional peppermint liqueur to splash in the soup.

6 to 8 servings

3	tablespoons margarine or butter
2	tablespoons canola oil
5	medium-sized leeks, trimmed, white part only, thinly sliced*
2	white, yellow, or Spanish onions, chopped
4	large Russet (baking) potatoes, peeled and sliced
3$1/2$	cups chicken broth
1	teaspoon salt (or less if broth is salty)
$1/4$	teaspoon freshly ground white pepper
3	cups milk
1$1/2$	cups half-and-half or evaporated skim milk
3	tablespoons (or to taste) peppermint liqueur
4	teaspoons chopped fresh mint for garnish

Heat margarine and oil in a large heavy saucepan or Dutch oven over medium heat. Add leeks and onions; cook, stirring often, until soft but not brown, 3 to 4 minutes. Add potatoes, chicken broth, salt, and pepper. Heat to boiling; reduce heat and simmer uncovered 30 minutes. Puree vegetables and broth in several batches in a food processor or blender; return to saucepan. Stir in milk, half-and-half, and liqueur. Heat but do not boil for 5 minutes, stirring often. Serve hot or cold garnished with chopped mint.

*See instructions for preparing leeks in the chart presented earlier in this chapter.

Sweet Mustard Leek and Sweet Potato Kabobs

Double-pronged skewers are available at cookware shops, department stores, and Gamatech, P.O. Box 8069, San Jose, CA 05155. Cook these kabobs at the same time you grill your main course.

6 servings

Sweet Mustard Marinade

1	cup light olive oil
1/3	cup red wine vinegar
2	tablespoons light brown sugar
1	tablespoon Dijon mustard
1	shallot, peeled and minced
1	teaspoon dried oregano
1/4	teaspoon garlic powder
1/4	teaspoon salt
1/4	teaspoon freshly ground pepper

3	medium-sized leeks, trimmed, white part only*
3	medium-sized sweet potatoes, peeled and cut into 1 1/2-inch cubes
	Canola oil for brushing grill rack

For Sweet Mustard Marinade, whisk olive oil, vinegar, sugar, and mustard in medium-sized bowl. Stir in remaining ingredients; reserve. Parboil leeks in lightly salted water, 3 to 4 minutes; drain. Cut leeks into 2-inch pieces. Parboil sweet potatoes until almost tender, about 15 minutes; drain. Combine vegetables and Sweet Mustard Marinade in a nonmetallic container. Let stand 1 hour at room temperature.

Prepare grill. Drain vegetables. Thread decoratively on six short, double-pronged skewers. Arrange skewers on oiled rack over glowing coals. Cook, rotating every 2 minutes until vegetables are tender and slightly charred, about 4 minutes or until done to taste.

*See instructions for preparing leeks in the chart presented earlier in this chapter.

Cockaleekie Tart

This recipe was inspired by the traditional Scottish soup made with leeks, potatoes, and chicken. The recipe also calls for prunes. We'd rather have the prunes for dessert.

6 servings

Single-Crust Pastry (see Index)

2	leeks, cleaned, including 1 inch green part, thinly sliced (about 3 cups)
$^1/_2$	pound red potatoes, peeled and diced (about 1 cup)
2	whole skinless, boneless chicken breasts, diced
1	cup water
3	eggs, slightly beaten
$^1/_2$	cup sour half-and-half
$^1/_2$	teaspoon salt
$^1/_4$	teaspoon freshly ground black pepper
	Leek leaf, cut into 5-inch strips, blanched

Prepare pie pastry as directed; roll into 12-inch circle on a lightly floured surface. Fit pastry in a 10-inch tart pan with removable bottom; trim edges even with sides.* Bake at 425 degrees until light brown, about 10 minutes; cool slightly. While pastry is cooking, place leeks, potatoes, chicken, and water in a medium-sized saucepan. Heat to boiling; reduce heat. Cover and simmer over medium heat 10 minutes; drain and reserve. Whisk eggs, sour half-and-half, salt, and pepper in a medium-sized bowl; stir into leek mixture. Pour leek mixture in tart shell; arrange leek strips in a spoke design on top. Place on a baking sheet and bake at 325 degrees until egg mixture is set, 20 to 25 minutes. Serve at room temperature.

*A 9-inch pie pan can be used instead of a tart pan with removable bottom.

Garlic Croutons

If you'd rather, you can bake the croutons in the oven.

5 to 6 servings

6	slices day-old dark bread, crusts removed
4	tablespoons ($1/2$ stick) margarine or butter, or a combination
5	cloves garlic, minced
$1/4$	teaspoon freshly ground pepper
$1/4$	teaspoon dried sage

Tear or cut bread into 1-inch cubes. Heat margarine in a medium-sized skillet; add garlic, pepper, and sage. Cook until garlic is hot but not brown. Sauté bread pieces in garlic butter, turning often with a spatula, until golden brown, about 5 minutes. Drain on paper toweling. Good warm or cold, sprinkled on salads.

Elephant Garlic Game Chips

Serve with roast pheasant or other game birds, grilled fish, or over a salad of wilted endive, thinly sliced boiled potatoes, and a hearty sherry vinegar-based dressing.

4 servings

2 cups canola oil
8 cloves elephant garlic, thinly sliced lengthwise
Salt

Heat oil to 375 degrees in a medium-sized saucepan. Slide about half of the sliced garlic into the oil. Cook until crisp, about 30 seconds. Remove with slotted spoon; drain on paper toweling. Repeat until all chips are cooked. Sprinkle with salt.

Baked Whole Heads of Garlic

Serve baked garlic as an appetizer, right out of the oven. Pass a bottle of good-quality olive oil to sprinkle on thinly sliced French bread, then spread the savory baked garlic on the bread. Baked garlic is also good added to mashed potatoes.

4 servings

4	firm heads of garlic, not separated into cloves, outer paperlike skin removed
1/4	cup olive oil
1/2	teaspoon dried oregano

Place garlic in a small baking pan. Brush with oil and sprinkle with oregano. Bake at 375 degrees until garlic is soft when squeezed, about 40 minutes. To serve, cut each garlic head in half horizontally. Let guests squeeze soft garlic pulp onto bread.

FOUR

BEETS

Beets are an underutilized root vegetable that deserve more attention. They are easy to cook and have a nice crisp texture and great color. They are nutritious and delicious. Beets have more natural sugar than any other vegetable. Beet greens contain some calcium and iron and more than enough vitamin A for a day in a serving.

Beets have long played a starring role in ethnic and regional cuisines. The Scandinavians eat beets in salads, sandwiches, soups, and even meatballs. Eastern European cooks stuff them into dumplings and use them for colorful, full-flavored borscht. Beets appear on Middle Eastern tables mixed with yogurt and exotic spices. Italians roast beets.

In our own country, New Englanders mix beets with leftover corned beef for Red Flannel Hash. Midwesterners mix beets and apples. Pickled beets are one of the "seven sweets and seven sours" served on Pennsylvania Dutch tables, and the Amish make a bright red beet jelly. Old-time cookbooks often have a recipe for beet wine.

Many traditional beet recipes combine sweet and sour ingredients—brown or white sugar and vinegar or lemon juice, for instance. Test this principle yourself. Combine tart apples and beets with a sweet dressing for a wonderful salad. Glaze cooked beets with butter and sugar, then stir in freshly grated sharp Parmesan cheese. Good cooks know that they have to adjust the sweet or sour to complement the natural flavor of the vegetable.

If you buy fresh beets with their tops intact, look for nice, fresh green leaves. Remove the greens as soon as you get home since they will draw flavor from the beets if left on.

The first rule of beet cookery is to cook whole beets unpeeled, with root and about 2 inches of stem attached. Avoid breaking the skin so that the beet juice will be sealed inside. Scrub them well with a brush, then wrap in foil and bake at 425 degrees for about 1 hour, or boil like a potato. Cooking time varies depending on the size and age of the beet. After cooking, let them cool until you can comfortably slip the skins off. They can then be diced, sliced, or quartered. Beets cooked in this way retain their bright crimson color and lose minimal amounts of vitamin C and potassium.

The second rule of beet cookery is to wear an apron to protect against the indelible juice of a peeled beet (raw or cooked). If you are combining beets with other ingredients and *want* the color to leech out (as in Pineapple-Orange Beet Relish or Hot Borscht and Smetana), then peel the beets first.

If you want some interesting table conversation, warn your family and friends that you are serving them anthocyanin—that's the natural red pigment in beets!

Baked Beets with Yogurt and Chives

Have you ever tried baking a fresh beet in the same style that you would bake a potato? Try this recipe! A baked beet is sweet, soft, and tasty. On a grill, rotate the beets every 10 minutes until tender, about 40 minutes, depending on the size of the beet and heat of the grill.

6 servings

6	large beets, about 2$\frac{1}{2}$ pounds, trimmed
1$\frac{1}{2}$	cups plain nonfat yogurt
$\frac{1}{2}$	cup chopped chives
	Salt
	Freshly ground pepper

Wrap each beet individually in aluminum foil. Bake at 425 degrees until tender, about 1 hour. Let stand until just cool enough to handle. While beets are cooling, combine yogurt and chives; spoon into a serving bowl. Unwrap beets; with fingers and a paring knife, slip off skins and trim. Mash or cut in half; serve rewrapped in fresh foil if you wish. Baked beets are best served hot. Serve with yogurt mixture, and let each person season to taste with salt and pepper.

Harvard Beets with Apples and Currants

Their crimson color no doubt explains how beets came to be associated with Harvard. Here we've brazenly updated the traditional New England recipe for Harvard Beets.

4 to 6 servings

1	bunch beets, peeled and trimmed
1	tablespoon cider vinegar
1	large Golden Delicious apple, peeled and thinly sliced
$1/2$	cup dried currants
4	teaspoons cornstarch
2	teaspoons grated orange zest
$1/4$	teaspoon ground allspice
$1/4$	teaspoon ground nutmeg
1	cup freshly squeezed orange juice
3	tablespoons margarine or butter
1	tablespoon honey

Place beets in a medium-sized saucepan; cover with lightly salted water. Heat to boiling; add vinegar. Reduce heat; cook covered over medium heat until tender, 35 to 45 minutes. Drain, reserving $1/4$ cup of the liquid. Slice beets into a serving bowl; stir in apples and currants. Reserve. In the saucepan, combine cornstarch, orange zest, allspice, and nutmeg. Stir in reserved beet juice, orange juice, margarine, and honey. Heat to boiling, stirring constantly, until mixture thickens. Pour over beet mixture; serve warm.

Beet Flan with Greens

Substitute or add fresh spinach if beet greens are not adequate. At the farmer's market, we ask for extra greens that other shoppers have had cut off.

8 servings

4	medium-sized beets, cooked, peeled, and cut up*
3	eggs
1	cup milk
4	tablespoons (1/2 stick) margarine or butter
2	tablespoons all-purpose flour
2	tablespoons sugar
1	teaspoon baking powder
1/8	teaspoon ground nutmeg
	Beet greens and/or fresh spinach, trimmed
	Salt
	Freshly ground pepper
	Nonstick vegetable spray

Place all ingredients except beet greens and salt and pepper in a blender or food processor; cover and blend. Pour into a 5- or 6-cup ring mold well coated with nonstick vegetable spray. Bake at 325 degrees until firm, about 30 minutes. Remove and let stand 5 minutes. Wash greens but do not drain; place in a large heavy saucepan or Dutch oven. Cover and cook, stirring once or twice, just until tender, about 3 minutes. Drain and press out excess moisture. Place on a cutting board and chop with a large knife; season to taste with salt and pepper. To serve, carefully unmold beet ring onto a serving plate; spoon cooked greens into the center.

*See the instructions given at the beginning of this chapter.

Pink Pasta with Mint

When Barbara's youngest daughter Dorothy was 10 years old, she asked for a pasta maker. She quickly became adept at pasta making. Here is one of her innovations.

6	medium-sized beets, cooked and peeled
1	cup instant flour plus extra to coat dough
1	cup all-purpose flour plus extra for sprinkling pastry board
$1/2$	teaspoon salt
$1/2$	teaspoon freshly ground pepper
1	extra-large egg
6	tablespoons olive oil, divided
	Flour for rolling out dough
3	tablespoons cider vinegar
1	large onion, thinly sliced
2	cups plain nonfat yogurt
$1/4$	cup minced fresh mint
	Freshly ground pepper

Place two of the beets in a food processor. Cut remaining beets into julienne strips; reserve cut beets. Puree the beets using the steel blade; add 1 cup of the instant flour, 1 cup of the all-purpose flour, salt, and pepper. Process until mixed, 8 to 10 seconds. Add the egg and 4 tablespoons of the oil; process 15 seconds to knead dough. Remove dough from processor and shape into a ball; sprinkle with instant flour. Cover with plastic wrap or aluminum foil and let stand at room temperature 25 to 30 minutes.

Knead dough on a lightly floured board 1 minute. Divide dough into quarters. Roll each piece through a pasta machine according to the manufacturer's directions, or roll thin with a rolling pin. Use a little all-purpose flour for surfaces if dough is sticky. Dry noodles 20 to 30 minutes on paper towels or use a pasta tree. Bring 4 quarts of water to a boil in a large kettle; add remaining 2 tablespoons oil and the vinegar. Cook noodles 1 minute; drain. Place cooked noodles on individual serving plates. Surround with cut beets and sliced onion. Mix yogurt and mint; spoon over pasta. Give each serving a quick grind of fresh pepper. Good hot or cold.

Hot Borscht and Smetana

We couldn't decide whether to do hot borscht, which is somewhat unusual, or cold borscht. So we did them both! For a smetana, or topping, use sour cream or plain nonfat yogurt.

8 servings

3	tablespoons canola oil
1	large onion, sliced
1½	pounds lean chuck, cut into ³/₄-inch pieces
2	bunches beets, peeled and thinly sliced
3	cups sliced red cabbage
¼	cup red wine vinegar
½	teaspoon salt
¼	teaspoon freshly ground pepper
2	large bay leaves
	Sour cream or plain nonfat yogurt

Heat oil in a large kettle or Dutch oven over medium heat. Sauté onion, stirring occasionally, for 3 minutes. Add meat; brown. Add beets, cabbage, and enough water to cover entire mixture. Stir in vinegar, salt, pepper, and bay leaves. Heat to boiling; reduce heat. Cook uncovered over medium heat until meat is tender, about 1 hour and 15 minutes. Discard bay leaves. Serve hot with a dollop of sour cream or yogurt, if desired.

Cold Borscht with Potatoes and Smetana

You know the wonderful sensation of a warm apple pie with ice cream? Now, try cold beet soup with hot mashed potatoes à la mode.

8 servings

2	pounds beets, peeled and sliced
3	tablespoons sugar
2	tablespoons freshly squeezed lemon juice
1/2	teaspoon salt
	Hot mashed potatoes
	Sour cream or plain nonfat yogurt

Place beets in a large kettle or Dutch oven; cover with water. Heat to boiling; reduce heat. Cover and simmer over medium heat until beets are tender, about 30 to 45 minutes. Stir in sugar, lemon juice, and salt. Puree beets with cooking liquid; cover and refrigerate. Serve cold with hot mashed potatoes and a generous dollop of sour cream or yogurt.

Beet Fruit Salad with Raspberry Vinegar Dressing

6 servings

6	Boston or radiccio lettuce leaves
1	small honeydew or cantaloupe melon, peeled and thinly sliced
1½	pounds beets, cooked, peeled, and sliced*
1	medium-sized red onion, sliced
	Raspberry Vinegar Dressing (recipe follows)

Raspberry Vinegar Dressing

½	cup olive oil
¼	cup raspberry vinegar
1	teaspoon honey mustard
¼	teaspoon salt
¼	teaspoon freshly ground pepper
1	cup low-fat cottage cheese or crumbled goat cheese

Arrange lettuce on six salad plates. Set melon and beets on lettuce; arrange onion on top.

Combine ingredients for dressing; drizzle over salad. Sprinkle cheese in the center of each salad. Serve chilled.

*See the instructions given at the beginning of this chapter.

Wilted Beet Garden Salad with Oranges and Capers

Beet greens have calcium and some iron, in addition to vitamin A. In this salad, the vitamin C in the oranges increases the absorption of iron from the beet greens.

4 servings

	Greens from 1 bunch of beets, washed, trimmed, and cut into bite-sized pieces
1/2	cup canola oil
1/2	cup red wine vinegar
1	teaspoon light brown sugar
1/4	teaspoon salt
	Freshly ground pepper
1	tablespoon capers, drained
1	8-ounce can sliced water chestnuts, drained
2	oranges, peeled and separated into segments

Blanch beet greens in lightly salted boiling water for 10 seconds; drain. Arrange greens on four salad plates. Whisk oil and vinegar together in a small bowl; whisk in sugar, salt, and pepper. Drizzle dressing over greens. Scatter capers equally over greens. Arrange water chestnuts and orange segments on greens. Serve cold or at room temperature.

Pickled Beets

Pickled beets are a real old-time American favorite. Anne's grandmother often served noodles with buttered crumbs and a dish of pickled beets for supper. Anne and her sister always vied for the tiny pink center ring of onion in the beets.

6 servings

2	cups cider vinegar
3/4	cup sugar
1/2	teaspoon salt
1	teaspoon pickling spice
3	bay leaves
1 1/2	pounds whole baby beets (or larger beets, sliced), cooked and peeled*
1	white onion, thinly sliced and separated into rings

Combine vinegar, sugar, and salt in a medium-sized nonaluminum saucepan. Tie pickling spice and bay leaves in cheesecloth; add to vinegar mixture. Heat to boiling. Add beets and onion; return to boiling. Remove from heat; remove spice bag. Spoon beets, onion, and juice into a bowl. Refrigerate covered at least 8 hours. Good as a garnish, salad, or vegetable side dish.

*Two 8 1/2-ounce cans whole baby beets, drained, may be substituted for fresh beets.

Pineapple-Orange Beet Relish

Here's an updated version of pickled beets. It's wonderful with pork or poultry. If cranberries are in short supply, substitute this relish.

4 cups

3	medium-sized beets, peeled and diced (about 2 cups)
1	large onion, diced
1	cup golden raisins
1	20-ounce can pineapple tidbits in juice (juice reserved)
1	orange
1/4	cup packed light brown sugar
1/4	cup cider vinegar
1/2	teaspoon salt
1	teaspoon black peppercorns, tied in cheesecloth

Place beets, onion, and raisins in a large heavy nonaluminum pan. Drain pineapple, reserving juice, and add to beet mixture. Remove orange peel in long thin strips with a peeler. Cut peel into tiny thin pieces; add to beet mixture. Squeeze juice from orange and add to reserved pineapple juice; add water, if necessary, to measure 2 cups. Stir juice mixture and remaining ingredients into beet mixture. Heat to boiling; reduce heat. Cook over low heat, stirring frequently, until mixture thickens, about 1 hour. (It will get thicker as it cools.) Remove peppercorns. Store covered in refrigerator.

Braided Beet Bread with Poppy Seeds

This bread is a lovely shade of pink. Use it for a sandwich of leftover New England Corned Beef (see Index).

2 loaves

¹/₂	cup vegetable shortening
2	¹/₄-ounce packages active dry yeast
³/₄	cup sugar
1	tablespoon salt
1	cup water
1	cup milk plus 1 teaspoon for topping
3	medium-sized beets, cooked, peeled, and quartered*
3	eggs, divided
8 to 9	cups all-purpose or bread flour
	Flour for rolling out dough
2	teaspoons poppy seeds

Combine shortening, yeast, sugar, and salt in a large mixing bowl. Heat water and 1 cup of the milk to 105 to 115 degrees; stir into shortening mixture. Let stand until yeast bubbles. Puree beets with two of the eggs in a blender or food processor; add to yeast mixture. Gradually add enough flour to make a stiff dough. Turn onto a floured board or knead with electric mixer until smooth and elastic, about 10 minutes. Place in a large greased bowl; turn to grease top. Cover and let stand in a warm place until double in size, about 1¹/₂ hours.

Punch down dough. Let stand 5 minutes. Divide into two parts. Form each part into three strips, 14 to 16 inches long. Place strips next to one another on work surface. Braid strips, beginning in the middle. Tuck ends under. Place each braid on a greased baking sheet. Cover and let stand until double in size, about 1 hour.

Heat oven to 350 degrees. Beat remaining egg with 1 teaspoon milk. Brush tops of braids with egg mixture; sprinkle with poppy seeds. Bake at 350 degrees until loaves sound hollow when tapped on the bottom, about 1 hour.

*See the instructions given at the beginning of this chapter.

FIVE

CARROTS

Our mothers used to say that if we ate our carrots, we'd have curly hair. Centuries ago, mothers in Afghanistan fed carrots to their children to make them righteous! But by the Middle Ages, mothers believed that eating carrots loosened sexual instincts and warned their sons and daughters about the inherent dangers of the phallic vegetable.

Before carrots were welcomed to respectable tables, they were considered a medicinal weed. Until the 17th century, carrots were prescribed for everything from diarrhea to dog bites. Anyone who gardens recognizes the descendants of those ancient roots that are now so hard to remove from cultivated beds. Carrotlike weeds include the beautiful but pesky Queen Anne's lace and the less common poison hemlock.

During the Renaissance, carrots were introduced to the table of Elizabeth I by a Dutch nobleman. The roots were cooked and eaten with butter; the women wore the fernlike foliage in their hair. Carrots quickly became a part of Anglo-Saxon cooking. The Pilgrim fathers and mothers brought carrot seeds with them to the New World. The dependable roots helped get them through the long hard winters. Native Americans were so taken with the new vegetable that they frequently stole them from the settlers' gardens.

Until recently, carrots have been considered a common, plain vegetable. They were used primarily in stews and soups, cut into sticks for a low-calorie snack, or served in an overcooked combination with peas. Anne's mother used to burn the carrots so often that the family came to prefer them that way! ''They were kind of caramelized,'' she says.

Carrots do have a long and noble tradition in Eastern European, Dutch, Belgium, and French cuisines. They also play an important role in Middle Eastern cooking. Carrots, along with other vegetables, were used more in countries where there were religious restrictions against eating meat. Russian Orthodox Christians feast on carrot pancakes before they enter the somber pre-Easter period. On special holidays, Jews prepare a dish of sweetened carrots and dried fruit. Some of our recipes are updated versions of these traditional ways to prepare and serve carrots.

Very young carrots can simply be scrubbed with a strong brush. To remove the bitter outer skin of most carrots with minimal loss of nutrients, scrape the carrots or peel with a sharp peeler. Replace peelers as they become dull.

Bright crisp foliage is an indication of freshness, but remember to remove the leaves immediately because they drain moisture from the carrots. Use the fresh greens as a garnish, as part of your centerpiece, or in your hair as did the ladies of Queen Elizabeth's court.

Carrot Jam

Carrot Jam is served as a relish with turkey or chicken. Make extra jars of jam to use as gifts. Add 2 tablespoons candied ginger for a slightly different taste.

Four 1-cup jars of jam

4$^{1}/_{2}$	cups peeled grated carrots
4	tablespoons freshly squeezed lime or lemon juice
$^{3}/_{4}$	teaspoon ground cinnamon
$^{1}/_{4}$	teaspoon ground nutmeg
1	cup dried currants

Cook carrots in lightly salted water until tender; drain. Combine carrots, lime juice, cinnamon, nutmeg, and currants in a large saucepan. Heat to boiling over medium heat, stirring frequently. Reduce heat and simmer uncovered, stirring often, until thick, about 30 minutes. Pour hot jam into sterilized jars and seal according to the manufacturer's instructions.

Individual Carrot-Prune Custard Molds

These individual carrot molds make a gleaming presentation. Garnish the top with a sprig of Italian parsley, if you wish.

6 servings

6	¹/₂-cup custard cups or shaped pastry molds
	Margarine or butter, at room temperature
12	pitted prunes
1	egg plus 2 egg whites
2	cups pureed cooked carrots
1	12-ounce can evaporated skim milk
¹/₂	teaspoon salt
¹/₂	teaspoon freshly ground white pepper

Brush molds with margarine or butter. Put two prunes in each mold; set aside. Preheat oven to 350 degrees. Slightly beat egg and egg whites in a medium-sized mixing bowl. Stir in carrots, milk, salt, and pepper. Ladle carrot mixture evenly into prepared molds. Place molds in a baking pan large enough to hold them all. Fill pan with enough hot water to measure halfway up sides of the molds. Bake until a tester inserted in the center of mold comes out dry. Remove and let stand 5 minutes. Remove molds from water. Run a knife around the edges and gently unmold onto individual dishes. Serve hot or cold.

Carrot Wontons

Carrot wontons can be served as a side dish, drained and sprinkled with freshly grated Parmesan cheese, toasted pine nuts, and orange zest, as an appetizer with a light sauce or with horseradish, or as an addition to chicken soup.

18 wontons

4	tablespoons olive oil
3	cloves garlic, minced
1/4	cup minced scallion with tender green tops
1/2	teaspoon grated fresh gingerroot
1	cup cooked pureed carrots
1/2	cup mashed cooked potato
	Salt
	Freshly ground pepper
18	wonton wrappers
1	egg white, slightly beaten
	Boiling water or hot oil for deep frying

Heat oil in a medium-sized skillet over medium heat. Sauté garlic, scallion, and gingerroot 1 minute, stirring often. Stir in carrot puree and mashed potato. Season with salt and pepper to taste; remove from heat and cool.

Arrange each wonton wrapper with the point facing you. Spoon a scant teaspoon of the carrot mixture in the center. With egg white (or water), lightly moisten two edges of the wrapper. Fold over and tightly press edges together to seal. Repeat until all are filled. Cook 2 minutes in a large skillet of gently boiling water over medium-low heat, or deep-fry if you wish. Remove with a slotted spoon or spatula; drain on paper toweling.

Baby Carrots with Green Grapes

6 servings

1	pound whole baby carrots
4	tablespoons ($^1/_2$ stick) margarine or butter
5	tablespoons honey
2	teaspoons freshly squeezed lime juice
$^1/_2$	teaspoon salt
$^1/_2$	teaspoon anise seeds
$^1/_4$	teaspoon freshly ground pepper
3 to 4	cups small seedless green grapes

Cook carrots in lightly salted boiling water just until tender, about 20 minutes; drain. Melt margarine in a medium-sized skillet. Add carrots; stir to coat with margarine. Stir in honey, lime juice, salt, anise seeds, and pepper. Mix with grapes; spoon into a serving dish.

Vichy-Style Carrots

Leave it to the French to devise a recipe calling for spring water bottled in Vichy! Vichy, or U.S. bottled water flavored with peaches, gives this classic dish a subtle flavor nuance. Serve more of the water with the meal.

6 to 8 servings

2	pounds carrots, peeled and cut diagonally into thin slices
4	tablespoons (¹/₂ stick) margarine or butter
1	tablespoon sugar
¹/₄	teaspoon salt
¹/₄	teaspoon dried tarragon
¹/₄	teaspoon freshly ground pepper
¹/₄	cup chopped chives
¹/₂	cup Vichy or peach-flavored bottled water
3	cups sliced fresh peaches for garnish

Cook carrots in boiling salted water 3 minutes; drain. Put under cold water 1 minute to stop the cooking. Heat margarine in a large skillet. Drain and add carrots; stir to coat with margarine. Sprinkle with sugar, salt, tarragon, pepper, and chives. Pour in bottled water. Heat to boiling; reduce heat and cook uncovered until liquid cooks away and carrots are tender, about 5 minutes. Serve hot, garnished with peaches.

Quail with a Mostly Carrot Mirepoix

A mirepoix is a combination of cooked, chopped root vegetables that are used in stews and stuffings or as a vegetable garnish. This recipe is good as a first course or luncheon dish.

4 servings

Mirepoix

3	tablespoons margarine or butter
1¹/₂	cups diced carrots
1	cup diced turnips
1	cup chopped onion
¹/₂	teaspoon dried tarragon leaves
¹/₄	teaspoon salt
¹/₄	teaspoon freshly ground pepper

Quail

4	whole quail, washed and patted dry
4	teaspoons olive oil or melted margarine
¹/₂	teaspoon garlic powder
	Salt
	Freshly ground pepper

For the mirepoix, melt margarine in a large heavy skillet. Sauté vegetables over medium heat, stirring occasionally, 10 minutes; season with tarragon, salt, and pepper. Cool slightly.

Set quail on a baking sheet. Brush with olive oil or melted margarine. Sprinkle with garlic powder and salt and pepper to taste. Stuff quail with mirepoix. Spoon any extra mirepoix into a baking dish. Bake quail and stuffing at 375 degrees until quail are golden brown and joints move easily, about 40 minutes. Serve hot.

Carrot Blini with Fresh Tomatoes and Dill Yogurt

Easter is the highlight of the Russian calendar. The week before Lent is a time of carnivals, parties, and eating contests. Blini with butter, jam, and smoked fish is traditionally served during the week-long festival that precedes the 40 somber days before Easter. Blini made with wintered carrots is traditional, but fresh tomatoes in early spring are a reality of modern American supermarkets.

About thirty 3-inch pancakes

1	pound carrots, peeled and chopped
1	medium-sized onion, chopped
1	cup water
1³/₄	cups all-purpose flour, divided
¹/₄	cup bulgur or whole-wheat flour*
1	¹/₄-ounce package rapid-rising yeast
1	teaspoon sugar
¹/₂	teaspoon salt
2	cups milk
2	tablespoons margarine or butter
2	eggs
1	medium-sized tomato, chopped
1	cup plain nonfat yogurt
1	tablespoon fresh dill *or* 2 teaspoons dried dillweed
	Nonstick vegetable spray

Cook carrots and onion in water in a medium-sized saucepan until tender; remove and cool slightly. Coarsely mash with a fork; reserve. Mix 1 cup of the all-purpose flour, bulgur flour, yeast, sugar, and salt in a large bowl. Heat milk and margarine until hot (125° to 130°F); stir into yeast mixture. Add eggs and carrot mixture. Gradually stir in remaining all-purpose flour. Cover and let stand in a warm place until double in size, 20 to 25 minutes.

Coat a large skillet with nonstick vegetable spray. Heat over medium-high heat until a drop of water sizzles on skillet. Make four or five pancakes at a time, using a scant $1/4$ cup batter for each. Cook until they begin to brown, about 4 minutes on each side. Do not undercook. Keep warm in a 250-degree oven. Serve warm with chopped fresh tomato and yogurt mixed with dill.

*Blini are traditionally made with bulgur flour, which is available in health food stores. Whole-wheat flour or an additional $1/4$ cup all-purpose flour can be substituted. Bulgur flour can also be made by grinding cracked wheat in a blender and then putting it through a coarse sieve.

Root Vegetable Fajitas

The Burton Stove Top Grill is a wonderful development in the art of grilling that allows you to grill indoors. Just set it on top of the stove, fill the reservoir with water, and grill!

4 servings

Fajita Sauce

1	tomato, finely chopped
4	tablespoons catsup
3	tablespoons canola oil
3	cloves garlic, minced
2	tablespoons freshly squeezed lime juice
$1/2$	teaspoon ground cumin
$1/2$	teaspoon chili powder
	Freshly ground pepper
	Salt
$1/2$	teaspoon liquid smoke (optional)
2	white onions, thinly sliced
4	carrots, julienned
1	red bell pepper, thinly sliced
4	flour tortillas

To make Fajita Sauce, combine tomato, catsup, oil, garlic, and lime juice in a small bowl. Stir in seasonings and liquid smoke. Brush onion, carrots, and red bell pepper generously with Fajita Sauce. If using a Burton Stove Top Grill, proceed according to the manufacturer's directions; if not, cook vegetables in a hot lightly greased skillet over medium heat. Cook, brushing occasionally with the Fajita Sauce and stirring occasionally until tender, about 4 minutes. Remove vegetables to a serving bowl. Heat tortillas on grill or skillet, about 20 seconds on each side. To serve, place a warm tortilla on each plate; add a portion of the grilled vegetables and roll up. Pass extra sauce.

Curried Carrots with Bananas

This exotic combination of flavors and textures gives the simplest roast beef, lamb, or chicken dinner an Indonesian aura.

6 servings

6	cups carrots, cut diagonally into slices 1/2-inch thick
2	tablespoons margarine or butter
1 1/4	teaspoon whole cumin seeds
1/2	teaspoon curry powder
1/4	teaspoon salt
1/2	teaspoon ground cardamom (optional)
1/2	cup golden raisins
2	bananas, cut diagonally into 1/2-inch slices
3	cups vanilla low-fat yogurt

Cook carrots in lightly salted water just until tender, about 20 minutes; drain. Heat margarine in a large skillet. Add carrots and stir to coat. Sprinkle with cumin, curry powder, salt, and cardamom. Cook and stir over medium heat. Add raisins and bananas; cook until heated through, about 4 minutes. Remove from heat and spoon into a serving dish. Top with vanilla yogurt. Serve hot.

Carrot Oatmeal Cookies

We recommend these for breakfast!

About 28 cookies

1/2	cup (1 stick) margarine or butter or a combination, at room temperature, cut into 1-inch pieces
1/3	cup granulated sugar
1/3	cup packed dark brown sugar
1	egg plus 2 egg whites
1	teaspoon vanilla
3/4	cup all-purpose flour
3/4	teaspoon baking soda
1/2	teaspoon ground cinnamon
1/4	teaspoon salt
13/4	cups quick-cooking rolled oats
2	cups peeled grated carrots
1/2	cup raisins

Preheat oven to 375 degrees. Cream margarine and sugars in a large mixer bowl with an electric mixer until light and fluffy. Beat in eggs and vanilla on medium speed. Gradually beat in flour, baking soda, cinnamon, and salt. Mix in remaining ingredients on low speed. Drop by rounded tablespoons onto a lightly greased baking sheet, 2 inches apart. Bake until firm and edges are golden, 15 to 20 minutes. Cool 1 to 2 minutes before removing to a wire rack to cool completely.

Carrot Cake

This recipe comes from Mary Abbott Hess, a registered dietitian and wonderful cook. She believes that healthful food should taste great and look beautiful. After meeting Mary, Julia Child wanted to join the American Dietetic Association, of which Mary was then president.

10 to 12 servings

1¹/₂	cups all-purpose flour
1¹/₂	cups sugar
1¹/₂	teaspoons baking powder
1	teaspoon baking soda
1	cup canola oil
3	eggs
2	cups peeled grated carrots (about 6 large carrots)
1	8-ounce can crushed pineapple, drained
¹/₃	cup chopped walnuts or pecans
	Cream Cheese Frosting (recipe follows)
1	cup walnut or pecan halves for garnish

Preheat oven to 350 degrees. Combine dry ingredients in a large mixing bowl. Add oil and eggs; beat with an electric mixer on medium speed until combined. Add remaining ingredients, beating on low speed just until mixed. Pour into greased and floured (or coated with vegetable oil with flour spray) bundt, springform, loaf, or 8-inch cake pans. Bake until center of cake is firm, 45 to 50 minutes. Let cool 30 minutes; remove from pan and cool completely on a wire rack. Frost with Cream Cheese Frosting, and garnish with walnut or pecan halves, if desired. Store cake, covered, in the refrigerator.

Cream Cheese Frosting

1	8-ounce package Neufchâtel cheese, at room temperature, cut into small pieces
6	tablespoons ($^3/_4$ stick) margarine or butter, at room temperature, cut into small pieces
3$^1/_2$ to 4	cups sifted confectioners' sugar
1$^1/_4$	teaspoons vanilla

With an electric mixer, beat cheese until light in a large bowl. Beat in margarine. Add confectioners' sugar, 1 cup at a time, until mixture is smooth and spreadable. Beat in vanilla.

SIX

JICAMA AND JERUSALEM ARTICHOKES

It's time we rediscovered jicama and Jerusalem artichokes. They're low in all the things we're supposed to cut back on, like fat and sodium and calories. They're healthy but not boring!

Texture rather than taste distinguishes jicama. It has an intriguing crunch and juicy white flesh that is similar to an apple. It maintains its crisp texture even when it's cooked. Add julienne strips or cubes of jicama to salads, side dishes, stir fries, and even a fruit salad. Your guests will be trying to guess the mystery ingredient.

The bland flavor of jicama allows the vegetable to absorb subtle flavors of dressings, marinades, and seasonings. Sprinkle it with lime juice, chili powder, and coarse salt in the Latin style, and serve with an icy drink.

Spanish explorers discovered jicama in Mexico and South America and carried it to southeast Asia and China. There, it is known as "yam bean." Yam bean appears in many dishes. In Thailand, the versatile root is dyed with food coloring, coated with cornstarch, fried until crisp, then served for dessert, topped with sweetened coconut milk and sesame seeds. Will yam bean perhaps be the ice cream flavor of the month one day?

We have to admit that before we began working on this book, neither of us knew much about Jerusalem artichokes. We were surprised to learn that they are indigenous to this country. Native Americans introduced colonists to Jerusalem artichokes. Even earlier, in 1605, the explorer Champlain reported eating the strange roots on Cape Cod. Samples were sent back to Europe, and the plant became popular in Italy and France. James Beard writes that Jerusalem artichokes grow wild along French roads. *Topinambours*, as they are called, appear on many French menus in soups, salads, and side dishes.

"Jerusalem artichoke" is a misnomer. The root is not from the Holy Land and is not related to the artichoke. "Jerusalem" is a corrupt form of the Spanish *girasole* or Italian *girasol*, meaning "sunflower." Indeed, Jerusalem artichokes are sunflower roots. It's unfortunate that the more descriptive names, "sun root" and "sunchoke," have not been adopted. As for the "artichoke" description, to some people the vegetable has a flavor and texture that resembles the globe artichoke. We think the sweet starchy root is more like a potato.

In fact, Jerusalem artichokes can be prepared like potatoes: boiled, roasted, fried, creamed, and put into soups, salads, and casseroles. Recipes for pickled Jerusalem artichokes date back to the 17th century and appear in many cookbooks, especially in New England, South Carolina, and Pennsylvania Dutch country.

Jerusalem artichokes are distributed September through June, primarily by Frieda's Inc. (1950 East 20th Street, Los Angeles, CA 90058), a specialty produce distributor. The tubers, which look like fresh ginger, will keep a week in the refrigerator.

To prepare, give the roots a brisk scrub with a stiff brush. Use them unpeeled or rub off the thin skin after cooking. To prevent raw Jerusalem artichokes from discoloring, put them into a bowl of water with lemon juice. To keep them white during cooking, leave the peels on or add milk to the cooking water.

A word of caution: Some people experience flatulence (gas) from Jerusalem artichokes. Test your tolerance by eating a small amount if you aren't sure how your system will react.

Jicama and Avocado Salad with Pineapple Dressing

4 servings

1	7-ounce can pineapple in syrup
1/3	cup buttermilk or plain nonfat yogurt
1/2	teaspoon salt
1/4	teaspoon freshly ground pepper
1	pound jicama, peeled and cut into julienne slices about 1/4 inch by 1 inch (about 2 cups)
	Romaine lettuce, cut crosswise into thin strips
1	avocado, peeled and diced
1	lime

Place undrained pineapple, buttermilk or yogurt, salt, and pepper in a blender container or food processor. Process until pineapple is pureed. Pour into a medium-sized bowl; add jicama. Let stand 30 minutes, stirring occasionally. Arrange romaine on serving plates. Spoon jicama and pineapple mixture onto romaine. Place equal amounts of avocado on top of each salad. Cut four round slices from one half of the lime; reserve. Squeeze juice from the other half of lime over the avocado-topped salads. Garnish with reserved lime slices.

Grilled Jicama and Spicy Black Beans with Radish Salsa

Grilled jicama is great with chicken or beef. Serve with hamburgers as a healthful alternative to french fries. If you don't want to start up the grill, use your broiler.

6 servings

Grilled Jicama

1	tablespoon paprika
1	teaspoon salt
$1/2$	teaspoon sugar
$1/2$	teaspoon ground cumin
$1/4$	teaspoon freshly ground black pepper
$1/8$	teaspoon cayenne pepper
1	jicama, about 6 inches in diameter, peeled
2	teaspoons canola oil

Combine paprika, salt, sugar, cumin, black pepper, and cayenne pepper in a small bowl. Cut jicama into $1/2$-inch slices. (For easier handling, first cut jicama in half lengthwise, then cut each half in semicircular slices.) Place jicama slices in a single layer on a baking sheet. Brush with oil; sprinkle with half the spice mixture. Turn and repeat on other side. Transfer jicama slices to grill rack placed over medium-hot coals, grill 5 minutes on each side.

Spicy Black Beans

1	tablespoon canola oil
1	medium-sized onion, chopped (about $1/2$ cup)
1	large clove garlic, chopped
2	teaspoons chili powder
$1/4$	teaspoon ground cumin
$1/2$	teaspoon crushed red pepper flakes
1	$14^1/2$-ounce can whole tomatoes, undrained and crushed
2	15- or 16-ounce cans black beans, drained

Heat oil in a large heavy skillet. Sauté onion and garlic in oil until tender, about 5 minutes. Stir in chili powder; cook and stir 2 minutes. Stir in remaining ingredients. Cook over medium heat, stirring occasionally, 10 minutes.

Radish Salsa

8	ounces radishes, trimmed and grated (about 2 cups)
3	tablespoons sugar
3	tablespoons white vinegar

Grate the radishes by hand or in a food processor. Combine ingredients in medium bowl. Drain and serve with Grilled Jicama and Spicy Black Beans.

Sante Fe Stir-Fry

Jicama is a wonderful addition to this classic southwestern combination of squash and corn. If you prefer, dice the zucchini and jicama. This is one of our favorite, and fastest, vegetable recipes.

6 servings

2	tablespoons canola oil
1	large onion, diced (about 1 cup)
1	zucchini, unpeeled and cut into 1/4-inch slices
1	cup corn, frozen or fresh
8	ounces jicama, peeled and cut into thin slices about 1 inch by 1 inch
2	tablespoons sunflower seeds
1	teaspoon salt

Heat oil in a large skillet over medium heat. Add onion; cook until onion is tender, 5 to 10 minutes. Stir in zucchini, corn, and jicama. Cook uncovered over medium heat, stirring occasionally, until zucchini is crisp-tender, about 5 minutes. Add sunflower seeds and salt.

Jicama Gazpacho with Shrimp

Serve this spa-type recipe in a clear, stemmed goblet for a light meal. Without the shrimp, the mixture makes a fresh-tasting, salsalike dip for large, restaurant-style tortilla chips.

6 servings

1	small jicama, about 12 ounces, peeled and cut up
1	green pepper, seeded and cut up
1	medium-sized onion, cut up (about $1/2$ cup)
2	small or 1 large clove garlic, cut up
1	$14^{1}/_{2}$-ounce can peeled tomatoes, undrained
1	6-ounce can tomato paste
2	tablespoons olive oil
2	tablespoons wine vinegar
3	drops Tabasco sauce
$1/2$	teaspoon salt
$1^{1}/_{2}$	pounds shrimp, cooked, peeled, and deveined
	Parsley for garnish

Place everything except the shrimp and parsley into a food processor. Process with on/off button until finely chopped but not pureed. Pour into a nonmetallic container; cover and refrigerate at least 12 hours. To assemble, reserve six shrimp for garnish; cut remaining shrimp into bite-sized pieces. Layer jicama mixture and shrimp pieces in glass goblets or sherbet dishes, using about $3/4$ cup mixture for each. Top with a reserved whole shrimp and parsley sprig. Refrigerate until serving time.

Baked Sunchokes with Orange Butter

6 servings

12	Jerusalem artichokes, well scrubbed
8	tablespoons (1 stick) margarine or butter, at room temperature
2	tablespoons grated orange zest
2	tablespoons freshly squeezed orange juice
1	teaspoon chopped chives

Pierce unpeeled Jerusalem artichokes twice with a fork. Place on a baking sheet and bake at 400 degrees until just tender when tested with the tip of a knife, 35 to 40 minutes.

While they are baking, combine margarine and remaining ingredients in a small bowl. (If made ahead, cover and refrigerate. Remove and let come to room temperature before serving.) Serve orange butter with hot split Jerusalem artichokes.

Jerusalem Artichokes with Steamed Greens

Early Boy Scout manuals give directions for digging wild Jerusalem artichokes, wrapping them in wet leaves, and cooking them in the camp fire. In the recipe below, eat the "leaves" along with the Jerusalem artichokes. Add bits of smoked ham, if you wish.

6 servings

1	pound Jerusalem artichokes, well scrubbed
2	tablespoons margarine or butter
1	large onion, chopped
2	pounds spinach, kale, chard, or other greens, well washed
2	tablespoons flour
1	tablespoon vinegar *or* freshly squeezed lemon juice
	Salt
	Freshly ground pepper

Cook Jerusalem artichokes in boiling salted water to cover in a medium-sized saucepan until tender when pierced with knife, 10 to 15 minutes. Drain and reserve. Heat margarine in the saucepan; add onion. Cook, stirring occasionally until tender; reserve. Place greens in a large heavy pot with just the water that clings to the leaves. Cover and steam, stirring occasionally, until wilted, about 5 minutes. Remove greens to a colander and press out all the water. Place greens on a cutting board; sprinkle with flour. Chop with a large knife until flour has been absorbed and greens are chopped. Add greens to cooked onion. Dice the reserved unpeeled Jerusalem artichokes and add to greens mixture. Cook and stir over medium heat until hot. Add vinegar or lemon juice and salt and pepper to taste.

SEVEN

HORSERADISH,
RADISHES,
PARSLEY ROOT,
AND CELERY ROOT

Horseradish is hot! And we aren't referring to taste alone. Amazing though it may seen, horseradish has become trendy. The most innovative chefs in the country are using horseradish to enhance lean meat and spark fresh vegetables and fruits. Many of their recipes are made with fresh horseradish root, not the bottled variety that's mixed with vinegar and salt.

Traditionally, the primary use of horseradish in this country has been with boiled and corned beef—that's still our favorite. Today, however, we're putting thin slices of fresh horseradish in beef and lamb stew, grating it into marinades, and mixing it with yogurt to coat baked fish and poultry. Horseradish is married to beets and onions, apples, and cranberries. It also spikes prepared mayonnaise, mustard, dips, and *wasabi*, a sauce served with sushi. Horseradish adds zip to bland cream sauces. It gives molded gelatin salads a new profile.

Horseradish tastes like something from another era, which it is. Centuries ago, it was used to relieve colic, remove worms, and reduce the effects of colds. It was given to sickly folk to stimulate the appetite. Horseradish is one of the lesser-known cruciferous vegetables that may help prevent cancer.

About 60 percent of the fresh horseradish in this country is produced in Collinsville, Illinois, on the Mississippi River near St. Louis. The rich, sandy soil is an ideal medium for the plant whose leaves grow waist-high.

Horseradish becomes milder with cooking. Keep a horseradish root in your refrigerator and grate it onto foods as you might add freshly ground black pepper. The root is odorless until the tissues are broken, releasing the mustard oils. Grating horseradish is like grating a strong onion, but thanks to the food processor, it's a quick and easy process now. Grate no more than you need, as it discolors quickly.

We think of radishes (the name comes from *radix*, meaning "root") as common and ordinary, but in ancient Greece, they were venerated. Athenian artisans crafted beets of silver, turnips of lead, and radishes of gold. Asian cultures continue to hold the radish in high esteem. In modern-day Japan, radishes are wrapped and presented as gifts. They are one of the more attractive members of the cancer-preventing cruciferous cabbage family. Next time you want to wish a friend ''Good health!'' give them a fresh bunch of red radishes instead of red roses!

Like horseradish, radishes also have mustard oils, located in the skin. Peeling reduces the sharp flavor; so does cooking. Radish-red is water soluble and leaks out when cooked. Steamed or stir-fried red radishes are pale pink with a surprisingly delicate flavor that needs little more than a dash of salt and pepper.

We're used to small, round red radishes and the less common but widely available white or ''icicle'' radishes. In addition, there are many varieties of Asian radishes. They can be more than 30 inches in diameter and weigh as much as 60 pounds! Their skins are green, red, purple, black, and white, and some have colored flesh as well. ''Beauty heart'' radishes, with pink, red, and white flesh, are carved into exquisite rose-, dahlia-, peony-, and butterfly-shaped garnishes. In northern China, beauty heart radishes are considered a fruit. In this country, the most widely available Asian radish is the Japanese daikon. The daikon radish has white skin and a long tapered shape. It is hotter in flavor than the white icicle radish. Add daikon along with carrots and onions to your next soup or stew.

Black radishes, which look more like turnips than radishes, are especially strong flavored. To tame, sprinkle them with salt after slicing or grating them; let them stand for an hour, then rinse and press out all the liquid. Or parboil them for 5 to 10 minutes before adding to dishes like egg salad or coleslaw. Unlike red radishes, the black-skinned variety maintains its color during cooking. Steamed black radishes, scored or spirally inscribed, make a stunning presentation.

If you're not sure which hairy root is celery root, scratch and sniff until you find one that smells like celery. Celery root, or celeriac, is a variety of celery that is cultivated for its root rather than its stalks. Developed from a wild species of celery by 17th-century botanists, celery root was a common vegetable in Europe by the end of the next century. Celery root remoulade is still a standard item on a French bistro menu.

Celery root can be eaten raw, but most people prefer it cooked or at least blanched. It can be baked, steamed, braised, or boiled. Celery root can be prepared like potatoes. It mashes to a smooth consistency and mixes to a creamy, tasty puree with the addition of a little milk or cream, margarine, and seasoning. After peeling it, put the celery root in cold water to which you've added lemon juice to keep it from turning brown. Since the porous flesh absorbs water, don't soak it for more than a few minutes. Sometimes celery root has a few leaves. If they're in good shape, include them in your dish or use them as a garnish.

Parsley root looks like a parsnip or a white carrot with ferny parsleylike leaves. It has an aromatic, herbal taste that lends itself to soups and stews. It is widely used in Germany, Holland, and Poland. What is used in this country is raised exclusively in New Jersey. We had no trouble finding it in local supermarkets.

Red Radish Salad with Radish Sprouts

4 servings

2	heads bibb lettuce, trimmed, cored, washed, and drained
1	bunch red radishes, trimmed and thinly sliced
1	large tomato, sliced
1/4	cup Greek (Calamata) or large ripe olives
1 1/2	cups plain nonfat yogurt
3	tablespoons red wine vinegar
1/4	teaspoon salt
1/4	teaspoon freshly ground white pepper
1/4	cup chopped fresh parsley
1	cup (or to taste) radish sprouts

Put drained lettuce leaves decoratively on four salad plates. Arrange radishes and tomato slices on lettuce. Sprinkle with olives. Combine yogurt, vinegar, salt, pepper, and parsley in a small bowl. Spoon a dollop of dressing over radishes and tomatoes. Sprinkle with radish sprouts. Serve chilled.

Japanese Chicken One-Pot Dinner

6 servings

3	cups chicken broth or water
1¼	pounds boned, skinned chicken breasts, thinly sliced
½	pound daikon radish, peeled and thinly sliced*
1	cup bean sprouts, rinsed and drained
1	cup sliced carrots
⅓	cup dry white wine
2	tablespoons light soy sauce
1	tablespoon mirin (Asian rice wine)*
2	teaspoons sugar
¼	teaspoon salt
¼	teaspoon freshly ground pepper
2	cups cooked whole-wheat noodles

Heat chicken broth or water to a boil in a large heavy saucepan. Add chicken and daikon; cook over medium heat 8 to 10 minutes. Add bean sprouts, carrots, wine, soy sauce, mirin, sugar, salt, and pepper. Simmer until flavors have melded and food is cooked, 5 to 10 minutes. Add cooked noodles; heat. Serve in a bowl.

*Available in Asian food stores or large supermarkets.

Japanese Radish, Carrot, and Green Onion Pickles

6 servings

1   medium-sized daikon radish, about ³/₄ pound, peeled and cut into 2¹/₂-inch matchstick strips*
2   medium-sized carrots, peeled and sliced
2   red bell peppers, seeded and sliced
1   bunch scallions, trimmed, split horizontally, and cut into 1¹/₂-inch strips
2   cloves garlic, mashed
1   teaspoon grated fresh gingerroot

Pickling Sauce

3   cups white vinegar
3¹/₄   cups sugar
1¹/₂   cups water
1¹/₄   teaspoons salt
¹/₄   teaspoon garlic powder

Mix radish, carrots, peppers, and scallions in a large bowl. Fill a large pot half full of water; heat to boiling. Add vegetables to boiling water; remove pot from heat and let vegetables stand slightly to cool. Drain well. Combine drained vegetables, garlic, and ginger; place in a sterilized jar.

To prepare Pickling Sauce, combine all ingredients in a medium-sized saucepan. Heat to boiling over medium-high heat. Pour over vegetables to completely cover them. Cover and refrigerate for 8 days. Serve chilled.

*Available in Asian food stores or large supermarkets

Fresh Green Radish Soup

Green radishes are about 2 inches thick and 8 inches long. They are tangy, with a potatolike texture when cooked.

6 to 8 servings

3	tablespoons canola oil
3	cloves garlic, minced
1	large onion, chopped
1½	quarts (6 cups) chicken broth
2	cups thinly sliced carrots
2	cups peeled, thinly sliced green radish*
½	teaspoon salt
¼	teaspoon freshly ground white pepper
¾	cup chopped fresh cilantro

Heat oil in a large saucepan over medium heat. Sauté garlic and onion, stirring often until onion is soft, about 4 minutes. Add chicken broth, carrots, and green radish. Heat to boiling over medium heat; reduce heat, cover, and simmer until vegetables are tender, about 30 minutes. Season with salt and pepper. To serve, ladle hot soup into bowls and sprinkle with cilantro.

*Available in Asian food stores or large supermarkets

The Ultimate Root Vegetable Soup

Soup is best the day after it's cooked. Remove and discard any fat that accumulates on the top. This soup is a complete meal in a pot.

6 to 8 servings

4½	pounds chicken, trimmed of excess fat and cut into pieces
½	cup peeled, sliced celery root
2	medium-sized onions, sliced
3	large carrots, peeled and sliced
1	medium-large parsnip, peeled and sliced
1	turnip, peeled and sliced
1	large parsley root, peeled and sliced
1	teaspoon (or to taste) salt
½	teaspoon freshly ground pepper
	Hot cooked rice or noodles

Arrange chicken and vegetables in a stock pot or other large pot. Cover ingredients with water. Heat to boiling; reduce heat and simmer uncovered for 2½ to 3 hours. Add more water if necessary to cover chicken and vegetables as they cook. Skim any foam that forms on top. Season with salt and pepper the last half hour of cooking. Refrigerate soup in the pot. Strain into a clean pot. Remove chicken from bones and add to stock. Cut up or puree vegetables and add to stock. Taste to adjust seasonings. Refrigerate, covered, at least 8 hours. Reheat and serve with cooked rice or noodles.

Grated Celeriac with Yogurt Curry Sauce

Make allowances for reduced size of celery root when you remove the tough outer skin. One medium-sized celery root yields about 3¹/₂ cups grated. This salad with its exotic sauce makes a nice first course, garnished with fresh pineapple wedges and served with toast points.

6 servings

3	celery roots, peeled and grated
3	tablespoons freshly squeezed lemon juice
3	cups plain nonfat yogurt
¹/₄	cup reduced-fat or fat-free mayonnaise
2	teaspoons grated lemon zest
³/₄	teaspoon curry powder
¹/₂	teaspoon coconut extract
¹/₄	teaspoon grated fresh gingerroot

Cook celery root in boiling water 2 minutes; drain. Place in a bowl of cold water mixed with the lemon juice; reserve. Combine yogurt, mayonnaise, and remaining ingredients in a medium-sized bowl. Drain celery root. Add drained celery root to yogurt mixture; stir to coat celery root with the yogurt curry mixture.

Parsley Root Soufflé with Apples

A perfect accompaniment to roast goose or pork roast. This soufflé can be prepared and refrigerated up to 4 hours before baking.

6 servings

1	pound parsley root, peeled and diced (about 4 cups)*
1	cup water
2	tablespoons margarine or butter
1	tablespoon all-purpose flour
1/3	cup evaporated skim milk or half-and-half
1	teaspoon sugar
1/4	teaspoon salt
1/8	teaspoon freshly ground pepper
3	eggs, separated
1	red apple, unpeeled
2	tablespoons chopped parsley root leaves or fresh parsley

Place parsley root in water in a medium-sized saucepan; cover and cook over medium heat until tender, about 20 minutes. Drain and mash (makes about 1¹/₂ cups); keep warm. Melt margarine in another medium-sized saucepan; stir in flour. Cook and stir over low heat 2 minutes; stir in milk. Cook, stirring constantly, until mixture thickens and boils, 1 to 2 minutes. Remove from heat; stir in sugar, salt, and pepper. Gradually add ¹/₄ cup hot mixture to beaten egg yolks; stir into remaining hot sauce. Cut three thin wedges from the apple; reserve for garnish. Coarsely grate remaining apple with peel. Add grated apple, parsley root tops, and reserved mashed parsley root to sauce. Cool to lukewarm.

Preheat oven to 400 degrees. Beat egg whites until stiff. Fold parsley root mixture into egg whites. Spoon into an ungreased 1-quart soufflé dish. Bake until top is golden, about 20 minutes. Serve immediately, garnished with reserved apple slices. Divide into serving portions with two forks.

*If parsley root has nice leaves, use in recipe preparation.

Celery Root Alfredo

You'll be surprised by the distinct flavor of the celery root in this aromatic pasta dish.

6 to 8 servings

1	tablespoon olive oil
1	medium-sized onion, diced (about 1/2 cup)
1	medium-sized celery root, 8 to 12 ounces, peeled and diced
1	cup water
1	12-ounce can evaporated skim milk
1/2	cup freshly grated Parmesan or Asiago cheese
1	teaspoon salt
1/4	teaspoon freshly ground white pepper
1	pound spaghetti or other pasta, cooked and drained
	Celery seeds

Heat oil in a medium-sized saucepan until hot; cook onion in oil until transparent, about 5 minutes. Add celery root and water; heat to boiling. Reduce heat; cover and simmer until celery root is tender, 10 to 15 minutes. Puree celery root and onion mixture in a blender, gradually adding evaporated milk. Blend until smooth. Return mixture to saucepan and heat just to boiling; stir in cheese, salt, and pepper. Combine celery root sauce with drained cooked spaghetti. Serve topped with a sprinkling of celery seeds.

White Grated Horseradish

Barbara's grandfather did not cook. His one assignment was to be in charge of grating the horseradish, and she remembers him sitting on the back porch to do so. Years later, when she had to grate the horseradish herself, she realized what a labor of love this was! Fortunately, she now has a food processor that will do the job in seconds.

1 cup

$^1\!/_2$ pound horseradish root, peeled and cut into 1-inch pieces
$^1\!/_2$ cup half-and-half

Place horseradish chunks in a food processor fitted with steel blade. Process until grated, about 1 minute. Let stand another minute. Remove cover carefully, away from your face, as the odor is very strong. Add half-and-half; process until combined. Spoon horseradish mixture into a bowl; cover and refrigerate. Stir before serving.

Option: For Red Grated Horseradish, add 3 tablespoons beet juice from fresh or canned beets.

New England Corned Beef with Root Vegetables and Horseradish Sauce

Mary Burns of the Illinois Department of Tourism is originally from Winthrop, Massachusetts. Her family's traditional Saint Patrick's Day dinner is corned beef, root vegetables, and horseradish.

6 to 8 servings

1	lean corned beef brisket, about 3½ pounds, trimmed of excess fat
1	large rutabaga, peeled and cut into cubes
2	small heads cabbage, about 1 pound each, cored and cut into wedges
8	new red potatoes, unpeeled
4	large carrots, peeled and sliced in half horizontally
2	turnips, peeled and cut into quarters

Horseradish Sauce

2	cups light sour cream or plain nonfat yogurt
¼	cup reduced-fat or fat-free mayonnaise
5	tablespoons White or Red horseradish (see preceding recipe)
2	teaspoons freshly squeezed lemon juice
¾	teaspoon sugar

Cover corned beef with water in a large pot. Heat to boiling over medium-high heat; reduce heat. Simmer, partially covered, 2 hours. Add rutabaga and cabbage; cook 10 minutes. Add remaining vegetables. Cook uncovered until meat is tender and vegetables are done, about 30 minutes. While meat and vegetables are cooking, prepare Horseradish Sauce: Combine sour cream with mayonnaise in a small bowl. Stir in remaining ingredients. Cover and refrigerate until ready to serve. Stir before serving.

When meat and vegetables are done, remove corned beef; let stand 5 minutes. Slice, against the grain, into thin strips. Place beef slices on a large platter and surround with drained vegetables. Serve hot with Horseradish Sauce.

Beet and Horseradish Salad

This salad looks especially nice on red radiccio and green lettuce leaves.

6 servings

1	bunch beets, cooked and peeled*
1/4	cup red wine vinegar
3/4	teaspoon caraway seeds
1/2	teaspoon salt
1/4	teaspoon freshly ground pepper
2	tablespoons capers, drained
2	tablespoons grated, peeled fresh horseradish
4	hard-cooked egg whites, chopped
1/2	cup regular, reduced-fat, or fat-free mayonnaise
	Lettuce leaves and radiccio

Cut beets into julienne strips; place in a medium-sized bowl. Stir in vinegar, caraway, salt, and pepper. Cover and refrigerate up to 4 hours; drain. Toss beets with capers, horseradish, egg white, and mayonnaise. Cover and refrigerate. To serve, mound beet mixture onto lettuce-lined salad plates.

*See the instructions for cooking beets given at the start of the ''Beets'' chapter.

Lumpy Mashed Potatoes
with Horseradish

4 servings (about ³/₄ cup each serving)

8	Round Red potatoes, 1¹/₄ to 1¹/₂ pounds, unpeeled
¹/₄	cup buttermilk
¹/₄	cup sour half-and-half
2	tablespoons (or to taste) grated fresh horseradish
¹/₂	teaspoon salt

Cook potatoes in boiling water to cover until fork tender, about 20 minutes. Drain; return potatoes to hot pan. Coarsely mash potatoes, including peels, with a fork. Gradually add buttermilk and sour half-and-half, mashing and stirring with a wooden spoon. (Potatoes will still be fluffy but somewhat lumpy). Stir in horseradish and salt.

EIGHT

TURNIPS,
RUTABAGAS,
SALSIFY,
AND PARSNIPS

Turnips and rutabagas are both members of the cabbage family, which means they are both cruciferous vegetables. Cruciferous vegetables, including broccoli, brussels sprouts, cabbage, horseradish, kohlrabi, radishes, and watercress, in addition to the turnip cousins, take their name from their crosslike flowers with four petals. Researchers are busy studying the role of these vegetables in preventing cancer. Don't wait until the evidence is all in to start eating them!

If you like foods with a sharp or peppery flavor—a little oomph—you'll like turnips and rutabagas. The flavor and odor comes from mustard oil. Mustard oil is bound to sugar in the raw vegetables but is activated by cooking. The longer you cook turnips and rutabagas, the stronger their flavor and odor.

Because of their distinctive flavor, turnips and rutabagas go well with robust foods like pork, pot roast, lamb shanks, and game. We think of them primarily as fall and winter vegetables, though they are available year-round. The first tender turnips, freshly plucked from the garden or purchased at a farm stand in August, are the very best. Preparation techniques are similar for rutabagas and turnips, except that rutabagas take a little longer to cook. They can be used interchangeably in recipes.

Turnips are best when they are about 2 inches in diameter. It's easy to tell when they get to this stage because they grow above the ground. The purple on them shows the earth line. Turnips are also grown for their leaves. Turnip greens, cooked with smoked pork and fresh chili pepper, are a traditional Southern dish. The juice of cooked greens, known as "pot likker," is a favorite tonic for a hangover. We can't vouch for their hangover effectiveness, but we will support the bone-building properties of the calcium in turnip greens.

Rutabagas are a cross between a turnip and cabbage. They were developed by a Swiss botanist in the 17th century. Unlike their ancestors, rutabagas grow underground. With their mottled yellow and purple skin, they're much coarser looking than turnips.

In times past, rutabagas and turnips were kept in root cellars in Northern climates. Rutabagas, which are heartier than turnips, were sometimes left in the frozen ground and dug up in the spring. Our refrigerators have a much higher moisture level than old-fashioned root cellars. Rutabagas can be stored for several months and turnips for no more than a week. In supermarkets, rutabagas are coated with paraffin to keep them from becoming dehydrated.

Parsnips, a member of the carrot family, are also a cold-weather vegetable. They are not harvested until after frost, which changes their starch to sugar. Their sweet flavor has spawned many creative uses. Combined with fruit and honey, parsnips were served in cakes to the Roman Emperor Tiberius. In Tudor England, parsnip flour was used for bread, and in the colonies there were parsnip-based cakes and puddings. During the Middle Ages, youngsters who were being weaned were given sweet parsnips to suck. The Irish have used parsnips to make beer. We suggest adding a parsnip to balance flavors of soups, spaghetti sauce, and braised meats.

Salsify, also known as oyster plant, was once common in this country and is still widely available in Europe. With the renewed interest in vegetables, it's making a comeback here.

There are two varieties of salsify, one white and one black. The white variety looks like a twisted carrot; the black variety is longer and more regular in shape. Don DeLuca, the produce manager of our local Dominick's supermarket, ordered it for us. We received a package of 16, long (12–15 inches), thin, black-skinned roots, weighing about 3 pounds. Not a word on the package was in English. Packed in Belgium, half the instructions were in French, the other half in German. The delicately flavored *schwarzwurzeln* (''black root'') is extremely popular in Germany. This black variety is known in Spanish as *scorzonera*, meaning ''black bark.''

White salsify, because of its uneven surface, is hard to peel before cooking. Fortunately, the thin skin is easily removed after cooking, if you don't overcook the root. Black salsify can be scraped or peeled before cooking, but the flesh turns brown immediately. As you peel the roots, drop them into a bowl of water to which you've added 2 tablespoons of lemon juice. Let the roots stand in the acidulated water for 10 minutes before cooking. We found that it was easier to scrub then boil them in their skins until just tender when pierced with a knife, 6 to 8 minutes. The skins came right off the cooled roots with a little help from a paring knife, exposing the bright ivory-white flesh.

If you are sensitive to gas-forming properties in foods, add a drop or two of Beano, a food enzyme, to cooked turnips, rutabagas, and salsify, or restrain yourself from second helpings until you've tested your system's tolerance.

Mashed Turnips and Pears

6 servings

5	large turnips, peeled and sliced
2	large ripe Anjou pears, peeled, cored, and chopped
3	tablespoons margarine or butter
$1/2$	teaspoon dried tarragon
$1/4$	teaspoon salt
$1/4$	teaspoon white pepper
2	tablespoons freshly squeezed lime juice
2	large ripe Anjou pears, cored and sliced for garnish

Cover turnips with water in a medium-sized saucepan. Heat to boiling; reduce heat. Cook uncovered over medium heat until turnips are tender, about 20 minutes. Drain and rinse under cold water. Mash drained turnips and chopped pears in a large bowl. Beat in the margarine, seasonings, and lime juice. Taste to adjust seasoning. Serve hot, garnished with the sliced pears.

Mashed Rutabagas with Peaches

Sweden is the rutabaga capital of the world—so much so that rutabagas have come to be known as "swedes." Native Scots ward off the Highland chills with "bashed neeps," a mixture of boiled rutabagas and potatoes. We've mashed our neeps and swedes with peaches for a uniquely American casserole.

6 servings

2	medium-large rutabagas, peeled and diced (about 6 cups)
1	large red potato, peeled and quartered
3	tablespoons margarine or butter
1	peach, (fresh or canned), peeled and pureed
1/4	cup half-and-half
1/3	cup fresh fine bread crumbs
1/2	teaspoon ground mace
1/2	teaspoon ground cinnamon
	Salt
	Freshly ground pepper
2	egg whites, beaten stiff
3	small peaches, (fresh or canned), peeled and sliced for garnish

Cook rutabagas and potato in boiling salted water to cover in a medium-sized saucepan until tender, about 25 minutes. Drain; mash. Stir in margarine, peach puree, half-and-half, and bread crumbs. Season with mace, cinnamon, and salt and pepper to taste. Fold in egg whites. Spoon into a greased 2-quart ovenproof casserole dish. Bake at 350 degrees until top begins to brown and vegetables are hot, about 30 minutes. Garnish with peach slices.

Turnips, Sweet Potatoes, and Couscous

To toast pine nuts, heat them in a nonstick pan for 5 minutes, stirring constantly. They will brown nicely. Serve this dish as a main course or as a side dish with lamb.

6 servings

4	tablespoons (¼ cup) olive oil
4	cloves garlic, minced
6	medium-sized turnips, peeled and quartered
3	medium-large sweet potatoes, peeled and quartered
1	small rutabaga, peeled and diced
1½	cups pitted prunes
2	cups chicken or vegetable broth
2	teaspoons ground cumin
½	teaspoon ground cinnamon
¼	teaspoon ground allspice
¼	teaspoon ground nutmeg
	Salt
	Freshly ground pepper
3	cups instant couscous
4	tablespoons (½ stick) margarine or butter
6	scallions with tender green tops, chopped
½	cup toasted pine nuts
½	cup dried currants

Heat oil in a large saucepan or Dutch oven over medium heat. Add garlic; cook and stir for 1 minute. Do not let garlic brown. Add turnips, sweet potatoes, and rutabaga; cook for 5 minutes, stirring occasionally. Stir in prunes, broth, and seasonings. Heat to boiling; reduce heat. Cook covered over low heat until vegetables are tender, about 30 minutes.

While vegetables are cooking, prepare couscous according to package directions. Make sure that you stir constantly to avoid lumps. Mix in margarine and scallions. Mound couscous on platter; surround with hot cooked vegetables. Sprinkle pine nuts and currants on top. Serve hot.

Rutabagas with Stewed Dried Fruit

4 servings

 3 medium-large rutabagas, peeled and diced (about 6 cups)
 1 8-ounce package mixed dried fruit
 1/2 cup sugar
 1 cup freshly squeezed orange juice
 2 tablespoons margarine or butter
 2 sticks cinnamon
 1 cup water

Parboil rutabagas in lightly salted boiling water in a medium-sized saucepan for 10 minutes; drain. Combine drained rutabagas, dried fruit, sugar, orange juice, margarine, and cinnamon in the saucepan. Stir in water. Heat to boiling; reduce heat, cover, and simmer over low heat until rutabagas and fruit are tender, 15 to 25 minutes. Good hot or at room temperature.

Pureed Rutabagas with Pan-Fried Leeks

For a richer taste, cook rutabagas in vegetable or chicken broth.

2	medium-large rutabagas, peeled and diced (about 6 cups)
6	tablespoons olive oil, divided
1	large leek, washed, trimmed, cut into thin pieces and separated into circles*
2	tablespoons margarine or butter, at room temperature
1/4	cup half-and-half
1/4	teaspoon ground nutmeg
1/4	teaspoon salt
1/4	teaspoon freshly ground white pepper

Cook rutabagas in lightly salted water to cover in a medium-sized saucepan until tender, about 25 minutes. While rutabagas are cooking, prepare leeks. Heat 4 tablespoons olive oil in a medium-sized skillet over medium heat. Stir-fry the leeks until dark brown; drain on paper toweling. Reserve. Drain rutabagas; puree them with margarine, the remaining 2 tablespoons of olive oil, half-and-half, nutmeg, salt, and pepper. Spoon or pipe rutabaga puree onto individual dishes; sprinkle leeks on top. Serve hot.

*To clean leeks, see the chart in the "Onions, Leeks, Shallots, and Garlic" chapter.

Russian Root Salad

For a traditional New Year's dish, soak a ¹/₂ pound of herring overnight in cold water; cut into strips, and add to salad with chopped hard-cooked eggs. We serve Russian Root Salad with cider-basted ham when we're having the whole family for dinner.

10 to 12 servings

2	large beets, cooked, skins and stems removed, and cut into ¹/₂-inch cubes (about 2 cups)*
1¹/₂	pounds red potatoes, peeled and cut into ¹/₂-inch cubes (about 3 cups)
¹/₂	pound carrots, peeled and cut into ¹/₂-inch cubes (about 2 cups)
3	turnips, peeled and cut into ¹/₂-inch cubes (about 1¹/₂ cups)
2	parsnips, peeled and cut into ¹/₂-inch cubes (about 2 cups)
1	cup peeled and diced celery root
³/₄	cup diced onion
2	tablespoons Dijon mustard
1	cup reduced-fat or fat-free mayonnaise
	Salt
	Freshly ground pepper

Place diced beets in a large bowl; reserve. Cook potatoes in boiling water in a medium-sized saucepan just until tender, about 8 minutes. Remove with slotted spoon; add to beets. Add carrots, turnips, and parsnips to the water in the saucepan; cook just until tender, 3 to 4 minutes. Remove with a slotted spoon and add to beet mixture. Add raw celery root and onion to beet mixture. Combine mustard and mayonnaise; add to beet mixture. Stir to combine. Cover and refrigerate. Season to taste with salt and pepper.

*To cook beets, see the instructions given at the start of the "Beets" chapter.

Root Risotto

Risotto makes a nice lunch, or serve it as a side dish.

6 to 8 servings

4	tablespoons olive oil
1	large onion, minced
3	cloves garlic, minced
1	cup uncooked long-grain rice
1	cup peeled, diced turnip
1	cup peeled, grated parsnip
1/2	cup peeled, grated carrot
1 3/4	cups chicken broth, divided
1/2	teaspoon salt
1/2	teaspoon freshly ground pepper

Heat oil in a large heavy skillet over medium heat. Cook onion and garlic, stirring occasionally, about 4 minutes. Stir in rice. Cook and stir until rice browns slightly, about 5 minutes. Stir in turnip, parsnip, and carrot. Add 1 cup of the chicken broth. Cover and cook 10 minutes. Uncover and stir; add remaining broth, salt, and pepper. Cover and continue cooking until rice is cooked and vegetables are tender, about 20 minutes. Serve hot.

Grilled Root Vegetables with Chive Polenta with Goat Cheese

A Griffo Grill is a most valuable tool. It fits directly on the grill and keeps small and soft pieces of food from falling through onto the coals. For best results, always use hardwood charcoal.

6 servings

Olive oil to brush pan, grill, and vegetables

Chive Polenta with Goat Cheese

1	quart boiling water
1/2	teaspoon salt
1	cup yellow cornmeal
1/4	cup chopped chives
1/2	teaspoon dried sage
	salt
1/4	teaspoon freshly ground pepper
1/4	pound plain goat cheese, crumbled

Grilled Root Vegetables

6	medium-large carrots, peeled, parboiled, and drained
6	medium-sized parsnips, peeled, parboiled, and drained
6	scallions with tender green tops
1	red onion, cut into 1/2-inch slices
1/2	teaspoon dried rosemary
1/2	teaspoon garlic powder
1/2	teaspoon dried thyme

¹/₄ teaspoon salt
¹/₄ teaspoon freshly ground pepper

Lightly oil a 9-inch-square baking pan; reserve. Bring water and salt to boil in a large heavy pot over medium heat. Pour cornmeal into water in a slow steady stream, stirring constantly with a whisk. Continue whisking as the cornmeal cooks. Add chives, sage, salt to taste, and pepper. Cook, stirring continually, until cornmeal thickens, 8 to 10 minutes. Pour cooked cornmeal into prepared pan. Smooth top. Cover and refrigerate until firm to touch, 25 to 30 minutes. Cut into nine 3-inch-square pieces. Split each square horizontally; spread with goat cheese. Replace top, making a polenta "sandwich." Place polenta sandwiches on grill rack with the vegetables (below); grill for 4 minutes, turning once. Polenta will be hot and the cheese soft.

Prepare grill. Cut carrots and parsnips in half or quarters. Brush vegetables and grill rack with oil; place on grill when coals are glowing. Arrange vegetables on grill; season with rosemary, garlic powder, thyme, salt, and pepper. Grill 3 to 4 minutes, turning once. Vegetables will be slightly charred and tender.

To serve, mound vegetables on a plate and set a polenta sandwich on the side of the vegetables. Serve hot. Pass extra polenta at the table for seconds.

Parsnips with Pineapple and Macadamia Nuts

Toast the macadamia nuts in a 325-degree oven for 10 minutes, stirring once.

6 servings

6	medium-large parsnips, peeled and cut in half
3	tablespoons margarine or butter
1/2	cup buttermilk
1	8³/₄-ounce can crushed pineapple in juice, drained
1/2	teaspoon lemon pepper
	Salt
1/2	cup chopped, toasted, unsalted macadamia nuts

Cook parsnips in lightly salted water over medium heat until tender, about 20 minutes. Drain; cut parsnips into 1-inch pieces. Mash parsnips with margarine and buttermilk. Stir in pineapple, lemon pepper, and salt to taste. Serve hot, sprinkled with macadamia nuts.

Scalloped Oyster Plant

New England cooks substituted salsify when oysters were not available; hence salsify became known as oyster plant. The texture of salsify is a little like oysters, and the plant is bland enough to pick up flavors from other ingredients with which it's combined. When Anne was testing this recipe, her husband, a Mayflower descendant who knows his scalloped oysters, said it smelled just like the real thing. We thought the salsify looked more like scallops than oysters and had a scalloplike texture.

6 servings

1½	pounds salsify, scrubbed
1½	cups crushed oyster crackers
6	tablespoons margarine or butter, melted and divided
1	teaspoon salt, divided
¼	teaspoon freshly ground white pepper, divided
1½	cups fresh fine bread crumbs
1	cup half-and-half
	Paprika

Cut long salsify roots into pieces that will fit into a large saucepan. Parboil salsify in boiling salted water until tender but still firm, 6 to 8 minutes; drain and cool slightly. Scrape off skins with a knife; cut salsify into ½-inch rounds; reserve. Combine oyster crackers with 4 tablespoons of the margarine. Spread half the oyster crackers in the bottom of a small shallow baking dish. Arrange half the salsify in a single layer on top of the oyster crackers; sprinkle with half the salt and pepper. Layer remaining oyster crackers and salsify; sprinkle with remaining salt and pepper. Toss soft bread crumbs and 2 tablespoons margarine; arrange on top of salsify. Pour half-and-half over crumbs. Sprinkle with paprika. Bake at 350 degrees until top is brown and liquid has been absorbed, about 45 minutes.

Virginia's Root Vegetable Pot Pie

Virginia Van Vynckt is a prominent food and nutrition writer, and we're lucky that she shared this recipe with us. "A good recipe for winter," Virginia says.

4 to 6 servings

1/2	ounce dried shiitake mushrooms
2	tablespoons olive or canola oil
1	cup parsnips, peeled and cut into 1/2-inch cubes
1	cup carrots, peeled and cut into 1/2-inch cubes
1	pound potatoes, peeled and cut into 1/2-inch cubes
2	leeks, white part only, finely chopped*
1/2	cup plus 2 tablespoons all-purpose flour, divided
1/2	cup water
2	tablespoons dry red wine
1	teaspoon mixed dried herbs (such as Italian seasoning or fines herbes or herbes de Provence)
	Salt
	Freshly ground pepper
1	cup whole-wheat flour
1/2	teaspoon baking powder
1/2	teaspoon baking soda
1/4	teaspoon salt
1/4	cup vegetable shortening
3/4	cup (approximately) buttermilk
	Flour for rolling out dough

Soak shiitake mushrooms in 1 cup warm water until softened, about 20 minutes. Remove shiitakes, squeezing excess liquid from them back into soaking liquid. Cut off and discard shiitake stems; thinly slice caps. Strain soaking liquid; reserve. Heat oil in a 10-inch ovenproof skillet; add mushrooms and remaining vegetables. Cook over medium heat, stirring frequently, until vegetables begin to brown, 7 to 8 minutes. Sprinkle with 2 tablespoons all-purpose flour; stir. Stir in shiitake liquid, $1/2$ cup water, wine, herbs, and salt and pepper to taste. Cook, covered, over low heat until potatoes are nearly tender, about 20 minutes. Add more water if necessary to make a fairly thick gravy.

Preheat oven to 425 degrees. Combine remaining $1/2$ cup all-purpose flour, whole-wheat flour, baking powder, baking soda, and $1/4$ teaspoon salt in a medium-sized bowl. Cut in shortening with a pastry blender or two knives until mixture is crumbly. Stir in enough buttermilk to make a soft, sticky dough. Knead two or three times on a heavily floured surface. Roll out into a 10-inch circle. Lay dough on top of vegetables in skillet. Cut two or three slits in the crust for steam to escape. Bake until crust is golden, 20 to 25 minutes.

*To clean leeks, see the chart in the "Onions, Leeks, Shallots, and Garlic" chapter.

Salsify with Wilted Greens and Tomato Concasse

Serve this colorful arrangement of vegetables as a first course or salad.

6 servings

1	pound salsify, scrubbed
3	tablespoons olive oil, divided
1	medium-sized onion, coarsely chopped
1/4	cup water
5	tablespoons balsamic vinegar, divided
1	bunch escarole, cleaned and cut up
1	teaspoon sugar
	Salt
	Freshly ground pepper
2	large tomatoes
1	yellow bell pepper, minced
2	teaspoons freshly squeezed lime juice

Cut long salsify roots into pieces that will fit into a large saucepan. Parboil salsify in boiling salted water until tender but still firm, 6 to 8 minutes; drain and cool slightly. Scrape off skins with a knife. Cut into pieces 4 inches long and about 1/4 inch thick (about the size of thin asparagus stalks). Heat a large heavy skillet over high heat; add 1 tablespoon of the oil. Add salsify to hot skillet. Cook in two batches, turning frequently, until slightly charred; remove and reserve. Add onion, water, and 1 tablespoon of the vinegar to the skillet. Cover and cook over low heat 2 minutes; add escarole. Cover and cook, stirring frequently, until escarole wilts, about 5 minutes.

Drain in a colander, pressing out the liquid; season with sugar and salt and pepper to taste; reserve.

To make tomato concasse, cover tomatoes with boiling water; let stand until soft and skins are loosened, about 5 minutes. Remove skins and seeds; finely chop tomatoes. Place tomatoes in a medium-sized bowl; add yellow bell pepper. Whisk together the remaining 2 tablespoons oil, 4 tablespoons vinegar, and lime juice. Add 3 tablespoons of the dressing to tomatoes and peppers; reserve remaining dressing. Add salt and pepper to tomato mixture to taste.

To serve, mold about $1/3$ cup drained tomato mixture in center of a large serving plate. Arrange about $1/2$ cup of the greens around the tomato mixture. Stack salsify strips around the greens. Drizzle about 2 teaspoons of the remaining dressing over salsify and greens on each plate. Serve at room temperature.

**CELEBRATING
OUR ROOTS**

Why not serve an entire meal of root vegetable dishes? Here are our menu suggestions. Vive la roots!

South of the Border Root Vegetable Fiesta

Grilled Jicama and Spicy Black Beans with Radish Salsa

Latin American Potato Soup with Corn and Avocado

Southwest Yam Muffins

Root Vegetable Fajitas

Elephant Garlic Game Chips

Mashed Potato Chocolate Cake

Root Harvest Table

Carrot Blini with Fresh Tomatoes and Dill Yogurt

Russian Root Salad

Flat Onion Bread

Virginia's Root Vegetable Pot Pie

Braided Beet Bread with Poppy Seeds

Sweet Potato Nut Bread

Carrot Jam

Carrot Cake and Ginger Ice Cream

Index